Empirical Models of Urban Land Use:
Suggestions on Research Objectives
and Organization

NATIONAL BUREAU OF ECONOMIC RESEARCH

Exploratory Report 6

Empirical Models of Urban Land Use: Suggestions on Research Objectives and Organization

H. James Brown, Harvard University

J. Royce Ginn, National Bureau of Economic Research

Franklin J. James, Rutgers University

John F. Kain, Harvard University

Mahlon R. Straszheim, University of Maryland

EXPLORATORY REPORT 6

NATIONAL BUREAU OF
ECONOMIC RESEARCH

New York 1972

Distributed by Columbia University Press
New York and London

Contents

Tables

Figures

Foreword

DURING THE PAST fifteen years or so the United States has experienced a burgeoning interest in metropolitan land-use–transportation studies. Virtually every major metropolitan area in the United States has undertaken such a study. Several areas have undertaken more than one.

The very first of these models were fairly primitive: forecasts of the demand for transportation facilities often were made by simply "factoring up" (i.e., increasing) observed demands for existing facilities. Slowly, the realization set in that patterns of metropolitan land use depended upon the design and extent of the transportation system; this led to studies of increasing complexity and cost. Today these efforts commonly cost several millions of dollars, and the national investment in them is consequently great. Many talented people and sophisticated techniques have been employed. It is an understatement to say that the techniques are evolving. Thus, in the six studies examined in this survey, a diversity and increasing sophistication of techniques is quite evident.

In this environment of rapid change, a survey of current developments seems warranted. As the authors of this survey point out, there has been an unfortunate lack of candid and complete communication among the persons involved. In part this is the result of the institutional structure within which these modeling efforts are carried out. An equally important explanation, however, has been the comparative newness of these studies and the great number of innovations they embody. Communication under conditions of extremely rapid and independent development is almost never satisfactory. Given the great investments in these models themselves, not to mention the much greater investments affected by their outputs, this lack of adequate criticism and understanding potentially could be enormously expensive.

Empirical tests of the adequacy of the models as simulations of the real world have also been insufficient—in fact, largely impossible. For practical reasons, discussion and criticism of the models, therefore, have had to be a priori.

Criticism of land-use–transportation models is too varied and abundant to be effectively summarized in the space of these comments. The authors concentrate primarily on an obvious weakness of current land-use modeling efforts: lack of convincing behavioral content. As the authors suggest, current models have been created in a policy planning environment which places enormous emphasis on producing forecasts. Adequate basic research on the processes underlying and creating the patterns being forecast has not been encouraged to any large extent. Understandably, in this environment basic research has remained by and large inadequate. The resulting models are mechanistic; their logic and theoretical bases are often impenetrable.

As with the earlier exploratory reports issued by the National Bureau,[1] this report should be regarded as simply suggestive and not as a final program of research. The survey reported in this volume is both the rationalization and the first product of an effort at the National Bureau to undertake some of the basic research necessary to the development of satisfactory metropolitan land-use–transportation models. Several interrelated studies are now under way at the Bureau in the area of urban economics, research that we hope will eventually result in a much more complete understanding of the metropolitan area as an economic unit. An example of these studies is a large-scale econometric analysis of household residential choice. In this the effects of many factors are being studied—workplace location, income, demographic variables (including racial characteristics), and the design of transportation systems—on the choice by households of residence type, neighborhood type, and location. On the basis of the econometric estimations of these relationships, we hope to construct a computer simulation model of this process. Others at the Bureau are studying the determinants of intrametropolitan manufacturing location choices, using time-series data which allow cohort analysis. Still others are investigating the effects of different fiscal arrangements on the behavior of local governments. Effort is also, being directed at achieving a better understanding of urban labor markets and their operation, including a study of the participation of minority groups in these labor markets. In all, these

---

[1] *Research in Securities Markets* (1946); *Research in the Capital and Securities Markets* (1954); *Suggestions for Research in the Economics of Pensions* (1957); *The Comparative Study of Economic Growth and Structure: Suggestions on Research Objectives and Organization* (1959); *Research in the Capital Markets* (1964).

studies range from investigations of patterns of migration to and among urban areas to studies of specifically intraurban phenomena.

This preliminary report or survey has been done by the staff specifically involved in the land-use modeling. It has benefited from the insights and cooperation of many researchers active in the field. Its audience should be, I think, not only men technically involved in this type of modeling but all those interested in current research into the determinants of the form of metropolitan change and growth. We hope that it can be of significant value to both researchers technically involved and sophisticated in this field and to interested lay observers.

JOHN R. MEYER

Acknowledgments

THIS MONOGRAPH WAS a product of the initial stages of a research project done at the National Bureau with the support of the U.S. Department of Housing and Urban Development. The aim of the project was the development of experimental models of the spatial relationships of urban land-use activities. Compiling this survey and critique seemed to us, and to the Department of Housing and Urban Development, a natural adjunct to our modeling activities.

It is impossible to separately identify the contributions of individual authors. Each of us was involved in the development of every part of the monograph. However, some suggestion of the general demarcation of responsibilities may be useful, both for the record and for the reader. Mahlon Straszheim made major contributions to Chapter 1, in which a general introduction to the structure of transportation planning models is given. James Brown and Franklin James concentrated their efforts on Chapters 2 through 8, where summaries of the structures of the six models surveyed are presented. John Kain contributed greatly to Chapter 9, which offers criticisms and suggestions for improvement in the techniques of land-use modeling. Royce Ginn made important contributions to all areas of the monograph.

Of course, the authors owe a great deal to a great many people. Special thanks are due to Raymond J. Struyk, Stephen P. Dresch, Gregory K. Ingram, and Irving R. Silver of the NBER staff reading committee, whose criticisms and suggestions were invaluable to the authors; and to the members of the Board of Directors' reading committee for this study: Wallace J. Campbell, J. Irwin Miller, and Boris Shishkin. In addition, William Goldner and Joseph Nathanson of the Bay Area Transportation Study, T. R. Lakshmanan and D. D. Lamb of the Consad Research Corporation, and I. J. Rubin and S. Thyagarajan of the Detroit Regional Transportation and Land-Use Study (TALUS) deserve thanks for the patience and tolerance they showed while introducing us to their modeling efforts. In addition, we owe special thanks to Gnomi Schrift Gouldin and Hedy D. Jellinek for their editing of the manuscript, to H. Irving Forman for the charts, and to Mrs. Mary Parker for excellent typing. Her skill and dependability made our work much easier.

This report is part of a larger investigation supported by HUD Grant Number NY-MTD-15, administered by the Office of Urban Transportation Development and Liaison, Division of Systems Research and Development. We wish to thank the sponsors for their generous support. They are not, of course, to be held responsible for any of the statements made or views expressed.

Empirical Models of Urban Land Use: Suggestions on Research Objectives and Organization

Introduction

THE EFFECTS OF urban and intercity transportation systems on the use of urban land have long been discussed and debated. Unfortunately, the relationship between transportation and metropolitan development remains very poorly understood. It is clear that urban transportation helps shape the spatial distribution of employment and residences. Further, transportation affects neighborhood patterns, land values, income distribution, and a host of other determinants of the overall quality of urban living.

As public awareness of the validity and importance of these effects has grown, transportation planners have been forced into a thicket of interrelationships. Fortunately, perhaps, as the realization increased that transportation facilities could be adequately analyzed only as a system, and that this system had important effects on the areas it served, the technological capacity to analyze and simulate important characteristics of complex systems also grew, primarily with the development of electronic computers. Consequently, over the last twenty years there has occurred an enormous expansion of activity devoted to the analysis of the interrelationship of urban transportation systems and the spatial dimension of many urban activities.

As a result of this effort, tremendous advances have occurred not only in the sophistication of the techniques employed to analyze the impact of transportation systems but also in the choice of effects to analyze. When first begun, transportation system studies were in fact highway system studies: research was limited to the effects of the highway system on the way people lived while motoring from point A to point B. Today, as the six models discussed in this survey make clear, the breadth of analysis attempted in contemporary transportation studies is enormously greater and more sophisticated. In fact, these studies can no longer be truthfully called transportation studies—they are land-use–transportation studies.

The rate of evolution of the models has not slowed, as the diversity of the recent models surveyed makes clear. The range of techniques used in these studies is very broad indeed; the range of ambitions is equally broad. One study, for instance, reports the intention to develop an apparatus that, when programmed to accomplish a final land-use configuration, will produce a consistent and efficient set of public policies which can attain the desired land-use pattern. Others set for themselves the somewhat more modest goal of projecting land-use patterns some number of years into the future, and planning a transportation system consistent with the land-use pattern. Only the latter structure is operational to date. But we believe that the trend in land-use–transportation studies is in the direction of the former.

We believe that in our survey of these models we have made two valuable contributions to this field. First, we present reasonably complete and accurate summaries of several current efforts in the field of land-use modeling. These summaries provide the interested layman with an introduction to activities in this field, and the land-use modeler with a survey of what has been done or attempted elsewhere. We believe that documentation of land-use–transportation studies has been unsatisfactory, in fact, that progress in this field has been impeded by lack of accessible information on what is being attempted elsewhere, and on which attempts have failed and which have succeeded.

The second contribution is in the form of what we hope is productive criticism of these models, as well as suggestions for possible improvements in current modeling techniques.

Finally, the authors believe that simulations of the relationships between land use and transportation systems, however much they are improved, will never produce transportation-system planning free of public disagreement and debate. As we have pointed out, transportation systems profoundly affect individuals and groups. In addition, by no means are the benefits and the costs of investments distributed jointly. Often their separate distributions are perverse, with an inverse relationship between benefits received and costs borne by individuals affected by changes in these systems. We do believe, though, that improved land-use models can be a very productive source of information in the debates that inevitably arise around transportation-system planning. It is our hope that, by clarifying the effects of public investment on the spatial configuration of urban areas, reliable land-use models will allow policy makers to employ these investments more effectively as policy tools.

An overview of the institutions and methodology of current transportation-land–use planning is presented in Chapter 1. Chapters 2 through 8 contain a more detailed study of land-use models developed for five major metropolitan areas. A critique of the current state of land-use modeling and some observations about organizing research and model building for transportation planning are presented in Chapter 9.

1

Land-Use–Transportation Planning Studies

INTRODUCTION

"COMPREHENSIVE" METROPOLITAN land-use–transportation studies have been conducted in virtually every U.S. metropolitan area since World War II. The earliest studies were unashamedly and unabashedly highway planning studies. More recently a variety of local pressures, as well as the increasing participation of the Department of Housing and Urban Development (HUD) in the planning process, have caused these studies to give greater emphasis to transit planning, although highway planning remains their predominant concern. In the twenty years following World War II, analytical methods used in the studies have grown in both complexity and sophistication. The six studies evaluated in Chapters 2 through 8 reflect this growth.

To forecast future traffic volumes, the earliest urban transportation studies simply multiplied existing traffic volumes by a constant growth rate. The inadequacy of this technique soon became clear, and transportation planners began to search for improved methods. One early elaboration permitted recognition of the wide variations in growth rates within the metropolitan areas and allowed some adjustment for the rapid growth in traffic caused by new development in suburban areas.

Soon thereafter a number of planners began to think of directly relating urban traffic to land use. They recognized that the number of trips originating in, or destined for, each part of the region depended on the amount and kind of activity (land use) located there. If these relationships were fairly regular and stable, the quantity of various kinds of land use could be a measure of both current and future urban travel. This concept became the basis of the land-use–transportation method that has been employed in all recent studies. The Detroit Area Transportation Study (1953) is widely regarded as a landmark in the development of this method. The Detroit study's principal contribution was the development of systematic quantitative relationships between travel and land use which, in combination with land-use forecasts, were utilized to predict future travel. The land-use–transportation model developed in that study has been used with minor conceptual modification and great elaboration by nearly every urban transportation study since that time. Mitchell and Rapkin's study[1] provided additional theoretical justification for the procedure, and was highly instrumental in insuring that the techniques received widespread adoption by other transportation studies.

THE "STANDARD" METHOD

The general conceptual framework developed for use in the 1953 Detroit study is illustrated in Figure 1. The survey of land-use modeling and forecasting, which is the primary subject of this report, relates to only the first of the six boxes portrayed in the figure. The discussion that follows illustrates the manner in which the land-use forecasting models to be discussed later relate to the overall method employed in the land-use–transportation planning studies.[2]

One of the most important characteristics of this methodology is the unidirectional relationship between land use and transportation assumed in the model. The location and intensity of land use affect transportation demand and determine the amount and location of transportation facilities. However, the model incorporates no feedbacks between transportation and land use. Transportation investments are assumed, implicitly, to have no effect on the location or intensity of land use. This aspect of the standard model has been widely criticized. Critics

[1] Robert B. Mitchell and Chester Rapkin, *Urban Traffic: A Function of Land Use,* New York, 1954.

[2] For a more extensive and complete discussion of the material in this chapter, the reader is directed to John R. Meyer and Mahlon R. Straszheim, *Techniques of Transport Planning, Vol. I: Pricing and Project Evaluation,* Washington, D.C., 1970, Chapters 7 and 8. See also Richard M. Zettle and Richard R. Carll, "Summary Review of Major Metropolitan Area Transportation Studies in the United States," Berkeley, November 1962; and John F. Kain, "Urban Travel Behavior," in Leo F. Schnore and Henry Fagin, eds., *Urban Research and Policy Planning,* Beverly Hills, 1967, pp. 161–92.

Figure 1
The Land-Use – Transportation Forecasting Model

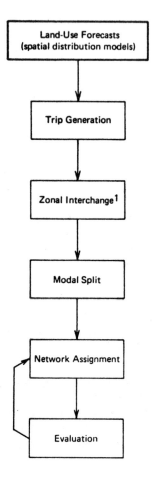

[1] In some studies zonal interchange and modal split are performed in the opposite order.

argue that land-use–transportation models may prove "correct" simply because they are self-fulfilling prophecies. Future urban travel may result from the transportation investments of the plan rather than from the future urban development as postulated by the model. Despite widespread dissatisfaction with this aspect of the model, no existing land-use model contains anything but the most trivial feedbacks of transportation investments on patterns of urban development. A fuller discussion of this question, particularly as it relates to the six land-use modeling efforts surveyed, is presented in later chapters.

Trip Generation

Transportation studies have probably devoted more time and more resources to the analysis of trip generation than to any other aspect of urban travel behavior. Trip generation refers to the number of trips produced per capita, per household, per acre, per worker, per dollar of retail sales, per square foot of floor space, or per other unit of land use.

The standard approach to estimating the number of trips originating in, or destined for, each area or zone is to assume that trip generation rates depend on the type and intensity of land use. Residential, commercial, and industrial land of various kinds usually generate a different number of trips per unit. The basic assumption of trip generation models is that the level of generation in each zone can be estimated by applying appropriate parameters for each specific class of land use. If these rates remain constant over time, and if land uses can be accurately forecast, the number of origins and destinations by zone can also be forecast accurately.

In particular applications, land area, employment, population density, and number of dwelling units have been used to estimate trip generation. The earliest land-use–transportation studies applied physical measures of land use, such as acres of land or square feet of floor space. Recent studies have stressed economic activity measures, such as employment, retail sales, and school enrollment.[3] A great deal of interest has focused on the development of behavioral trip-generation models for "home-based" trips (trips originating at or destined for

[3] For a brief survey of practices to date, see Paul W. Schuldiner, "Land Use, Activity, and Non-Residential Trip Generation," *Highway Research Record,* 141, Washington, D.C., 1966, pp. 73–88; B. C. S. Harper and H. M. Edwards, "Generation of Person Trips by Areas Within the Central Business District," *Highway Research Board Bulletin,* 253, Washington, D.C., 1960, pp. 44–61; Alan Black, "Comparison of Three Parameters of Nonresidential Trip Generation," *Highway Research Record,* 114, Washington, D.C., 1966, pp. 1–7; Paul H. Wright, "Relationships of Traffic and Floor Space Use in Central Business District," *Highway Research Record,* 114, Washington, D.C., 1966, pp. 152–68; and Donald E. Cleveland and Edward A. Mueller, *Traffic Characteristics at Regional Shopping Centers,* New Haven, 1961.

home). These models relate person or vehicle trips per household, per capita, or per dwelling unit to variables such as car ownership, net residential density, distance of the residence from the central business district, family income, and family size. Virtually every study has estimated a number of simple and multiple regression models that relate trips to one or more of these explanatory variables. While much has been learned from these analyses, a number of statistical and conceptual problems have been treated in a rather cavalier fashion and the nature of the underlying structure of these behavioral relationships remains unclear.

Zonal Interchange

Given an accurate forecast of the number of trips originating in, or destined for, each zone, the next step in the land-use–transportation procedure is to convert these origins and destinations into interzonal trips. Attempts to model zonal interchanges for urban areas almost always start by mapping the present interzonal flows. This requires an origin and destination survey. The earliest studies projected future interzonal travel by applying a constant growth rate to observed interzonal travel volumes. When the results of this crude procedure proved unsatisfactory, more sophisticated procedures were developed. The most widely used of the improved methods fall into three categories: the Fratar expansion method, the gravity model, and the intervening opportunities model.

The Fratar expansion method is a logical extension of the simple growth factor method.[4] It corrects the most obvious inadequacies of the growth factor model by allowing the rate of growth of interzonal travel to vary within the metropolitan area. In essence, the Fratar expansion method is an iterative technique that makes use of a different growth factor in each zone. Forecasts of interzonal travel are derived from the present level of interzonal trips and the different zonal growth factors. In an effort to incorporate more behavior into interzonal trip forecasts, transportation planners have moved from the Fratar method to other formulations.

The gravity model, in its simplest form, determines a set of flows from each point of origin to all other points (destinations). These flows

[4] T. J. Fratar, "Forecasting Distribution of Integral Vehicular Trips by Successive Approximations," *Highway Research Board Proceedings,* 33, 1954, pp. 276–384; and Walter Oi and Paul W. Schuldiner, *An Analysis of Urban Travel Demands,* Evanston, 1962, Appendix D.

are assumed to be directly proportional to the "attraction" at each destination and inversely proportional to the travel impedance (transportation cost or time) between the origin and the destination. Usually the travel impedance is some nonlinear function of the more direct measures of transportation cost. A typical formulation is

$$T_{ij} = P_i \frac{S_j A_j / D_{ij}{}^b}{\sum\limits_{k} S_k A_k / D_{ik}{}^b} \tag{1}$$

where

T_{ij} = the number of trips from origin zone i to destination zone j;

P_i = some parameter of the origin zone, such as the population;

A_j = some parameter of the destination zone, usually called the "attraction," and frequently reflecting floor area or acres of land;

D_{ij} = the direct measure of "distance" or transportation cost between the origin and the destination;

b = parameter, usually depending on trip purpose;

S_i = scalar determined from an iterative calibration procedure which requires $\sum\limits_{j} T_{ij} = P_i$ and $\sum\limits_{i} T_{ij} = A_j$, for those formulations where P_i is the number of trips "produced" and A_j is the number of trips "attracted."

The calibration of the gravity model is interpreted to be the determination of the parameter b, which is assumed to be invariant over time and therefore is a determinant useful in future trip distributions. The exponent b was consequently considered to be the only parameter to affect the distribution.[5] All other variables were either

[5] In situations where there is only one demand point or one supply point, the exponent can assume any positive value less than infinity with no effect at all on the resultant distribution. This is due to the requirement that $\sum\limits_{j} T_{ij} = P_i$ and $\sum\limits_{i} T_{ij} = A_j$. As the number of supply or demand points increase, the exponent begins to have an effect on the distribution. Since the attraction $(S_j A_j / D_{ij}{}^b)$ is standardized by the sum of the attractions as a denominator, the constant S_j will be unity when b is zero. When b assumes a nonzero value, this equation does not generate flows in such a way that the sum of terminating flows at every point is equal to the demand at that point. Hence, to maintain the equality of the sum of inflows to the demand at every demand point, S_j must assume a value different from unity.

measured directly or were forecast using standard trip generation techniques. When the value of the exponent is large (values of 2.5 typically have been associated with shopping trips), flows tend to be satisfied as close to the demand point (origin zone) as possible. A small value (the value of 1.0 is often associated with work trips) results in a more dispersed pattern. In the extreme, a zero exponent would allow demands (trip origins) to be satisfied at each destination in direct proportion to the per cent of the total supply (trip ends) available at the destination zone. The parameter b has been observed to vary between urban areas as well as between trip purposes.[6] More complicated formulations have been developed to account for some observed biases.[7]

Intervening opportunities, the third zonal interchange model in wide use, employs a stated probability of every destination being accepted. Total travel time is minimized for every origin, subject to the constraint that every potential destination is considered. Equations 2 and 3 summarize the intervening opportunities model. The expected interchange from zone i to zone j (T_{ij}) is the number of trip origins at zone i (O_i) multiplied by the probability of a trip terminating in j.[8]

$$T_{ij} = O_i[P(v_j) - P(v_{j+1})] \qquad (2)$$

or

$$T_{ij} = O_i\left(e^{-lv_j} - e^{-lv_{j+1}}\right) \qquad (3)$$

where

$P(v)$ = total probability that a trip will terminate by the time v possible destinations are considered;

v_j = "subtended volume," or the possible destinations already considered; that is, the trip destinations which could be reached before traveling far enough to reach zone j;

l = constant probability of a possible destination being accepted if it is considered.

[6] For a discussion of these differences, see J. Douglas Carroll and Howard W. Bevis, "Predicting Local Travel in Urban Regions," *Papers and Proceedings for the Regional Science Association,* 3, 1957, pp. 183–97.

[7] W. G. Hansen, "Evaluation of Gravity Model Trip Distribution Procedures," *Highway Research Board Bulletin,* 347, Washington, D.C., 1962, pp. 67–76; R. J. Bouchard and C. E. Pyers, "Use of Gravity Model for Describing Urban Travel: An Analysis and Critique," *Highway Research Record,* 88, 1965, pp. 1–43; U.S. Bureau of Public Roads, "Calibrating and Testing a Gravity Model in Any Size Urban Area," Washington, D.C., 1963, and "Calibrating and Testing a Gravity Model with a Small Computer," Washington, D.C., 1963.

[8] Morton Schneider, "Gravity Models and Trip Distribution Theory," *Papers and Proceedings of the Regional Science Association,* 5, 1959, pp. 51–56.

A trip originating in zone *i* thus has less probability of ending up in zone *j* as the number of intervening opportunities increases.[9]

The two terms in the brackets are, respectively, the probability of a trip getting to zone *j*, and the probability that, having reached zone *j*, the trip will not continue farther.[10] The parameter *l* shapes the distribution of interchanges, with a larger value of *l* leading to a more concentrated set of trips, given any surface of opportunities. Basically, the model allocates trips on an incremental basis over an opportunity surface rank ordered in descending fashion by travel time to the zone of origin, *i*.[11] Theoretically, the value of *l* is the slope of a log-linear relationship between the accumulated number of opportunities and the probability of continuing a trip. In practice, the relationship has not been linear and more than one *l* has been used in an additive form of the model.

Modal Choice

There are two basic approaches to modeling the number of trips that use various modes of travel in an urban area. These methods are generally referred to as "trip-end modal split models" and "trip-interchange modal split models." The names are derived from the particular variable that is "split" between modes. Each approach has its faults since the problem of trip frequency, destination choice, and mode choice is a simultaneously determined outcome in the real world.

Trip-end models were originally developed in conjunction with highway-oriented origin and destination studies, where they still have

[9] The mathematical formulation as the basis of this derivation is as follows:

$$dP = l\,[1 - P(v)]\,dv$$

where dP = probability that a trip will terminate when considering dv possible destinations. Other notation is as above.

The solution of this differential equation,

$$P(v) = 1 - e^{lv},$$

implies the equation in the text. (See Earl R. Ruiter, "Improvements in Understanding, Calibrating, and Applying the Opportunity Model," *Highway Research Record,* 165, Publication 1443, Washington, D.C., 1967, pp. 1–21.)

[10] Basically, the model premises a linear equation between the logarithm of the probability that a trip from zone *i* has not yet been satisfied by the time it "reaches" zone *j* $[1 - P(v)]$, and the number of intervening destinations or "opportunities" already considered by the time zone *j* is reached (v). The parameter *l* is the slope.

[11] Ruiter (see footnote 9) has attempted to explain the parameter *l* in behavioral terms of trip making. As a first approximation, *l* is related inversely to trip-end density and to the square of average trip length.

their most widespread use. As noted earlier, these studies are concerned primarily with forecasting automobile travel. In the simplest trip-end modal split models, some proportion of trips originating in each zone are simply subtracted from total trip generation before the remaining trips are assigned to the highway network. This transit-use proportion is often specified as a function of car ownership, net residential density, income, or a combination of these variables. An example of a modal split model of this kind is illustrated by equations 4 and 5:

$$F_i{}^b = \alpha_0 + \alpha_1 A_i + \alpha_2 D_i \tag{4}$$

and

$$F_{ij}{}^b = F_i{}^b \cdot T_{ij}, \tag{5}$$

where F_{ib} is the fraction of trips originating in i by mode b, A is auto ownership, and D is net residential density.

The most common elaborations of trip-end models have been the development of separate relationships by trip purpose. The purposes most commonly used in stratifying modal split models are school trips and work trips, since transit is generally more competitive with other travel modes for these purposes. Occasionally, special relationships are estimated for transit travel to and from the central business district (CBD) as identified separately from the remaining parts of the region, in recognition of the large differences in the levels of transit service to the CBD and to the remainder of the region.

Trip-interchange models initially were developed for transit feasibility studies, where they are still most widely used. The important characteristic of these models is that they emphasize comparative travel time, costs, and service by competing modes. The emphasis is easily understandable. A major rationale for transit feasibility studies is the diversion of current and future automobile commuters to transit as a result of service improvements.[12]

One of the most elaborate trip-interchange modal split models was developed in a transit feasibility study for the National Capital Transportation Authority in Washington, D.C. In this study, zonal interchange data for 1955 were stratified by trip purpose (work and nonwork), the ratio of highway trip costs to transit trip costs, the ratio of transit "service" to auto "service," and the median income of residence zones. One hundred and sixty subclasses were defined in this way.

[12] For a survey of these studies, see U.S. Department of Commerce, Bureau of Public Roads, Office of Planning, *Modal Split: Documentation of Nine Methods for Estimating Transit Usage*, Washington, D.C., December 1966.

Diversion curves, relating the per cent of transit usage to the ratio of highway travel time to transit travel time, were then obtained for each subclass.[13] Travel time ratios for work trips were based on peak hour conditions, while those for nonwork trips were taken from off-peak periods. The latter had to be applied to both peak and off-peak periods, which probably contributed to the poorer results in modeling nonwork trips.

The major result of this study is its suggestion of a much greater sensitivity of modal split to the performance of the highway system (parking delays and costs, and walking time) than to transit system performance. The model implies that a fifteen cent across-the-board fare increase (about a 50 per cent increase) would result in only a 5 per cent decline in total transit trips. This relatively low fare elasticity is consistent with other empirical studies. Changes in transit operating time were also judged to be of somewhat limited significance: for example, a 50 per cent rise in waiting and transfer time would reduce transit use by about 15 per cent.[14]

Network Assignment

The forecasts of interzonal travel by mode, obtained from the land-use, trip-generation, zonal interchange, and modal split models, are

[13] Thomas B. Deen, William L. Mertz, and Neal A. Irwin, "Application of a Modal Split Model to Travel Estimates for the Washington Area," *Highway Research Record,* 38, Washington, D.C., 1963, pp. 97–123; and Arthur B. Sosslau, Kevin Heanue, and Arthur J. Balek, "Evaluation of a New Modal Split Procedure," *Highway Research Record,* 88, Washington, D.C., 1965, pp. 44–63.

[14] Arthur Sosslau, Kevin Heanue, and Arthur Balek, "Evaluation of a New Modal Split Procedure," *Public Roads,* 33, April 1964, pp. 48–63.

Domencich and Kraft, in a substantial departure from this conventional planning format, suggested a model that treats trip generation, interchange, and modal choice simultaneously. Rather than let price or other service characteristics affect only the modal choice of a predetermined level of "directed" trips (i.e., origins and destinations are determined), they suggest including the influence of these characteristics on the level of trip making as well. After stratifying demand by trip purpose, their model fits an equation to zonal interchanges by each mode, and uses both transport system supply characteristics (such as travel cost or time) and basic economic variables (such as the type of land use, income levels, family size) as explanatory variables. See Thomas A. Domencich, Gerald Kraft, and Jean-Paul Valette, "Estimation of Urban Passenger Travel Behavior: An Economic Demand Model," prepared for presentation at the Annual Meeting of the Highway Research Board, January 1968.

finally "assigned" to proposed highway and transit networks as an initial stage in evaluating the adequacy of particular plans. Urban transportation studies have rapidly developed techniques for performing these assignments. The earliest assignments were restricted to limited freeway networks. They were made manually and were highly subjective. Typically, forecast interzonal traffic was divided between two alternatives (usually an existing arterial road and a proposed freeway), depending on relative travel time and distance. These assignments generally were based on "diversion curves," similar to those described previously for trip-interchange modal split models.

In 1957, a new era of network assignment modeling began as George B. Dantzig and Edward F. Moores independently developed a computer algorithm for finding the path through a network that would minimize travel time or cost.[15] The Chicago Area Transportation Study was the first to apply these techniques to urban transportation planning. Since 1957, development has been rapid and other studies have devised increasingly sophisticated assignment methods.[16]

The earliest "minimum path" assignment techniques assumed an infinite capacity for each network link. This, however, produced peculiar and unrealistic results: Because all traffic was assigned to "high performance" expressways, an "all-or-none" mapping was produced, either overloading links or assigning no traffic to them. The need for feedback between capacity utilization and link performance was quickly recognized.

In recent years, a number of techniques have been developed to incorporate capacity constraints. All use some form of iterative procedure in which continually updated travel times are used in the minimum path algorithms. For example, in the Chicago and Pittsburgh studies the network assignments were made one node at a time (a node is an entry or exit point on the network). Travel speeds on the network were adjusted each time to reflect the traffic previously assigned.

[15] George B. Dantzig, "The Shortest Route Problem," *Operations Research, 5,* 1957, pp. 270–73; and Edward F. Moores, "The Shortest Path Through a Maze," a paper presented at the International Symposium on the Theory of Switching, Harvard University, June 1957. Dantzig and Moores developed the solution independently of each other.

[16] Robert B. Dial, "A Probabilistic Multipath Traffic Assignment Model Which Obviates Path Enumeration," to be published in the 1971 *Highway Research Record* series.

2

Survey of Land-Use Modeling:
An Overview

INTRODUCTION

THIS CHAPTER CONTAINS reviews of six land-use models for five areas: (1) the Puget Sound Regional Transportation Study; (2) the Southeastern Wisconsin Regional Planning Commission Study; (3) the Atlanta Area Transportation Study; (4) the Detroit Regional Transportation and Land Use Study; (5) the Bay Area Simulation Study; and the (6) Bay Area Transportation Commission Study. Each of these models was designed to fit within the framework of a comprehensive study; that is, the models were developed with the broad problems of the area in mind even though they were specifically addressing only a small proportion of the overall problem. It is therefore useful to recognize the comprehensive objectives of the supervising agency.

Detailed individual descriptions of the six models are presented in subsequent chapters.

The goals of the studies, as stated below, are not necessarily those set forth in the enabling legislation or by specific agency directive, but more closely reflect the directions that were actually followed. This is partially so because in several studies the goals evolved while the project was under way.

For the Puget Sound study the major problem was one of developing a transportation network that would satisfy future demands for transportation. A reasonable estimate of future land-use patterns (with minor portions adjustable according to the transport services provided) was therefore required.

Two functional objectives coexisted in the Southeastern Wisconsin study. The short-run objective was the same as that for the Puget Sound study, with the additional purpose of providing information on the demand for schools, sewerage facilities, and housing construction. Scheduling was considered to be important, and therefore a series of incremental forecasts were used rather than a single-horizon forecast. The long-run objective was to develop techniques for producing the specification of land-use plans that would satisfy desirable development objectives and requirements at a minimum cost to the public sector. The costs to the private sector were also considered.

The objective of the Atlanta study was to design a transportation network that simultaneously permitted the solution of current problems and anticipated future requirements. A reasonable forecast of land-use patterns was necessary for estimating future transportation requirements.

The Detroit planners desired time-staged information (i.e., information over time) relating to future requirements for sewerage, schools, and other municipal services, as well as transportation requirements. It was recognized that locational choices by households and businesses would be affected by the supply of these services, which in turn would affect their future demand.

The objectives of the Bay Area Transportation Study (BATS) were to determine the general growth pattern of the region, the relation of land consumption to changes in employment locations, and the impact of several proposed transportation plans. The Bay Area Simulation Study (BASS) had similar objectives. The primary goal of BASS, however, was the development of techniques for studying a large variety of urban problems rather than simply the effects of transportation and employment location changes. Because of the similarity in major objectives and the dissimilarity in approach, we have included both the BATS and the BASS models in our review of land-use modeling for the Bay Area.

The spectrum of purposes is not very broad. However, the relatively small variance in the problems covered has had considerable effect on the modeling efforts. At one extreme, a study directed toward the satisfaction of transportation requirements forecast only the items directly relevant to that subject (i.e., population and industry characteristics directly related to trip-generation equations). At the other extreme, a study to develop a general set of planning tools focused on the complex relationships of industry and population location as a method of expanding knowledge in the field. Between these extremes were studies of other specific problems, such as the demand for schools, which in turn required forecasting the location of households, classified by life cycle, in order to project the number of children in each area.

THE MODELS

Figure 2 presents the basic structural linkages of the land-use modeling efforts of each study. The common allocation submodels are in the same relative position in each figure. The common framework includes forecasts of employment (EMP) and population (POP), and of the location of groups of industries (IND) and households (HOU). Most studies located retail (RETL) or service industries (SRVS) as separate categories, making them functions of the location of the basic industries and that of households.

In simplified form or schema, the approaches are remarkable for their similarity rather than their differences. Each of the models stresses the importance of industry employment location in determining household location, though they differ in the amount of reliance placed on employment location. In BATS, household location depends entirely on the place of work. By contrast, Southeastern Wisconsin relies more on the demand for particular kinds of housing and assumes that households will look for only a "reasonable" access to employment, retail services, and other households.

Retail employment is generally seen to adjust to household location. However, some approaches do not reflect this. BATS introduces a slight variance by locating retail service employment after the location of only basic employment households. In the cases of Detroit and BASS, retail employment is a function of the population locations in the previous time period, a feature made possible by their recursive approach to the simulation.

Since the location of basic industry is emphasized, it is annoying to find so little effort devoted to understanding the factors affecting the choice of industrial locations. In the extreme, the industries are simply placed where the planners would like them to locate. While this procedure is useful for studying the patterns conditional upon particular industry locations, it seems dubious to predict travel demand when no effort has been made to estimate the likelihood of that particular industry configuration. Even where industry location has been included in the study, the resultant models have not been particularly satisfactory.

Figure 2
Basic Structural Linkages of the Land-Use Models

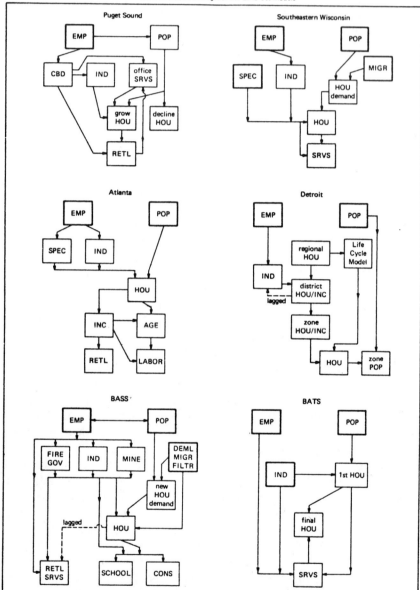

The figure also suggests the extent to which the models almost exclusively focus on the demand side of the housing market. The exceptions are BASS and Southeastern Wisconsin, which make quite different attempts to incorporate the supply side of the market. Still, it is not far from the mark to suggest that each of these models views the supply side of the market as simply reacting to housing demand.

Tables 1 through 7 below are presented as a cross classification of the techniques and the various submodels of the six models discussed in this paper, with Table 1 suggesting the general techniques used in each. The tables are included to enable the reader to make further comparisons of the similarities and differences among the models.

Tables of Land-Use Models

The purpose of these tables is to present a concise and certainly simplified picture of the overall workings and techniques used in the submodels of the six land-use models reviewed in this report. In Table 1 the submodels for each of the models are cross-classified with the most commonly used procedures or techniques. Tables 2 through 7 present the causality and relationships of the models. In each of these tables, the stub lists the various functions of the model, such as distribution of population, while the column heads at the top of the table list those factors upon which the functions of the model depend. The symbols in the body of these tables also require some explanation: An X indicates that the factor determining the function is exogenous to the land-use model. An E indicates that the determining factor is endogenous to the land-use model.

We have made every attempt to make these descriptions of the models as accurate as possible. Of course, any concise verbal description of analytical models as complex as these is a risky enterprise. We have tried as far as possible to follow the lead of the modelers and made large use of the published descriptions of their models. Our own choice of emphasis, however, will inevitably differ from that which they would have made.

Some aspects of these descriptions are quite technical. In most cases, the technical parts are not crucial for an understanding of the structure of the models. Further, the technical material is not important for understanding the evaluations made in the final chapter.

Table 1
Techniques and Procedures

	Regression	Judgment	Index Ranking	Gravity Access	Proration	Linear Program	Taxonomic	Un-specified	Trend
Puget Sound									
CBD employment projections									
Employment distribution, non-CBD areas								X	
Industrial							X		X
Retail									
Comparison goods		X						X	X
Convenience goods					X				
Office service	X								
Population distribution									
Growing areas	X	X		X					
Declining areas	X	X							
Southeastern Wisconsin									
Employment distribution									
Manufacturing		X				X	X		
Retail					X				
Special		X							
Population distribution				X		X	X		
Atlanta									
Industrial employment distribution			X						
Population distribution		X					X		X
Mean family income distribution		X					X		
Residential densities		X							

(continued)

Table 1 (concluded)

Spatial age distribution							X	
Distribution of labor force participation rates							X	
Retail sales space distribution	X			X				
Detroit								
Distribution of								
Employment	X	X		X				
Households to districts	X	X		X		X		
Households to zones	X							
San Francisco: BASS								
Employment distribution								
Distribution of								
Retailing	X	X		X		X		
Manufacturing	X	X			X			
Financial and real estate	X	X			X			
Services					X			
Construction	X				X			
Distribution of housing demolition and filtering					X			
Population distribution				X				
San Francisco: BATS								
Distribution of								
Basic industry to counties	X						X	
Basic industry to zones	X						X	
Basic industry employment families			X					
Population-serving employment			X					
Population-serving employment families			X					

Table 2
Puget Sound Regional Transportation Study

	Employment Projections		Non-CBD Employ-ment Totals	Land-Use Catalog	Regional Population Projections
	CBD	Regional			
Non-CBD employment totals	X	X	——	——	——
Distribution of non-CBD employment					
Industrial	——	——	X	X	——
Retail					
Comparison goods	X	——	——	——	——
Convenience goods	——	——	——	——	——
Office services	——	——	——	——	——
Population distribution					
Growing areas	——	——	——	X	X
Declining areas	——	——	——	——	——

Table 3
Southeastern Wisconsin Regional Planning Commission

	Regional Projections of		Soil Type Inventory
Distribution of	Employment	Population	
Industrial employment	X	——	X
Population	——	X	X
Special employment	——	——	——
Retail employment	——	——	——

Table 2
(concluded)

Distribution of				Housing Stock Charac- teristics	Trans- portation Measure
Industrial Employment	Population	Comparison Goods	Base-Year Office Services		
——	——	——	——	——	——
——	——	——	——	——	——
——	E	E	——	——	——
——	——	E	X	——	——
E	——	——	——	X	X
——	——	——	——	X	——

Table 3
(concluded)

Regional Design Plan	Distribution of		Transportation Measure
	Industrial Employment	Population	
X	——	——	——
——	E, X	——	X
X	——	——	——
——	——	E	——

Table 4
Atlanta Region Metropolitan Planning Study

	Area Projections			Distribution of		
	Employ-ment	Mean Family Income	Catalog of Land Uses	Industrial Employ-ment	Popula-tion	Mean Family Income
Industrial employment distribution	X	——	X	——	——	——
Population distribution	——	——	——	E	——	——
Mean family income distribution	——	X	——	——	E	——
Residential density	——	——	——	——	E	E
Spatial age distribution	——	——	——	——	E	E
Distribution of labor force participation rates	——	——	——	——	E	E
Distribution of retail sales space	——	——	——	——	E	E

Table 5
Detroit Regional Transportation and Land-Use Study

	Regional Projections			Lagged Distribution of	
Distribution of	Employ-ment	House-holds	Land-Use Catalog	Popula-tion	Employ-ment
Employment	X	——	E	E	E
Households to districts	——	X	E	E	E
Households to zones	——	——	E	E	E

Table 4
(concluded)

Spatial Age	Neighborhood Amenities	Housing Stock Assumptions	Tract Socioeconomic Characteristics	Transportation Measure
———	———	———	———	X
———	X	X	———	X
———	———	———	X	———
———	———	———	———	———
———	———	———	———	———
E	———	———	———	———
———	———	———	———	X

Table 5
(concluded)

District Amenities	Socioeconomic Characteristics of Population	Distribution of Households to District	Transportation Measure
———	———	———	X
X	E	———	X
———	E	X	———

Table 6
Bay Area Simulation Study

Distribution of	Regional Projections of		Catalogs of	
	Employment	Population	Land Use	Housing Stock
Retail employment	X	———	E	———
Manufacturing employment	X	———	E	———
Financial, real estate, and government employment	———	———	———	———
Service employment	X	———	———	———
Demolition and filtering	———	———	E	E
Population	———	X	———	E
Construction employment	———	———	———	———

Table 7
Bay Area Transportation Study

Distribution of	Distribution of Employment				Land-Use Catalog	Lagged County Rate of Growth
	Lagged	Basic to Counties	Basic to Zones	Nonbasic		
Basic industry						
Counties	E	———	———	———	E	E
Zones	———	E	———	———	E	———
Basic population	———	———	E	———	———	———
Nonbasic employment	———	———	E	———	———	———
Nonbasic population	———	———	———	E	———	———

Table 6
(concluded)

Initial Distributions of		Final Distributions of		
Employment	Population	Population	Employment Excluding Construction	Transportation Measure
E	E	—	—	X
—	—	—	—	X
	E	—	—	—
E	E	—	—	X
—	—	—	—	—
—	—	—	E	—
—	—	E	E	—

Table 7
(concluded)

Regional Projections		Population Distribution		Transportation Measure
Employment	Population	Base Year	Basic	
X	—	—	—	X
—	—	X	—	X
—	X	—	—	X
X	—	—	E	—
—	X	—	—	X

3

Puget Sound Regional Transportation Study

INTRODUCTION

A SCHEMATIC OVERVIEW of the procedure used in the Puget Sound study is shown in Figure 3. The sequence of operations is as follows:

1. Future aggregate levels of employment by industry and of population for the region are specified exogenously with the population forecasts disaggregated to the county level.

2. Regional population and employment forecasts are distributed to zones using a series of allocation models modified by a series of exogenous density constraints.

3. Further transportation requirements are computed for the forecast spatial distribution of households on the basis of their socioeconomic characteristics and the forecast distribution of jobs.

4. Increments to the highway system are then provided to satisfy projected travel demand.

The Puget Sound Regional Transportation Study evaluated two "alternative" land-use plans for 1990. Alternative land-use pattern A is a trend projection. In it a continuation of existing policies is assumed and, thus, a continuation of the changes in land-use characteristics during recent decades. Alternative plan B was chosen by the staff from five plans, each of which departed from existing trends in a different way. These five patterns could be achieved by appropriate zoning, open space, and transportation policies. They were (1) metrotowns—cities in the suburbs, each with a population of 100,000 to 300,000, linked with each other and with central cities by transportation facilities; (2)

Figure 3
Synthesized Flow Diagram for the
Puget Sound Area Land-Use Model

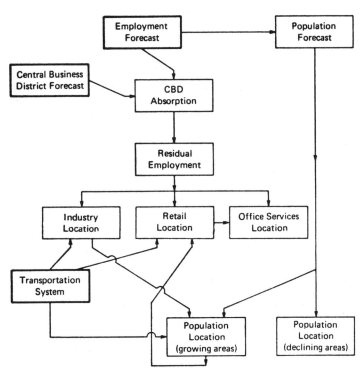

radial corridors—future development concentrated along principal transportation routes radiating from central cities, with the corridors of development separated from each other by wedges of green space; (3) linear corridors—development along the logical north-south transportation channels separated by belts of open space; (4) centralization —concentration of development in central cities, implying a maximum of commuting; (5) satellite towns—new development concentrated in planned suburban towns with populations of about 50,000. The radial corridors pattern was selected for testing as alternative plan B.

Future land-use patterns under plan B were to be achieved by modifying existing public policies. Thus, plan B projections are conditional on modifications in the transportation systems, changes in the zoning laws, and a vigorous program of acquiring open space designed to accomplish the radial pattern of development. In point of fact, the resulting land-use patterns are only marginally different under the two plans (for reasons detailed below).

METHODOLOGY

Aggregate Projections of Employment and Population

A sixteen-sector input-output model (fifteen sectors of manufacturing and one residual) was constructed for the Puget Sound region by the A. D. Little Company. The final demand vector depends on projected national growth in demand for the region's exports and projections of regional consumption, investment, and government spending. This final demand vector is then used to derive projections of the output of each regional industry. The sum of these forecasts of output by industry is the total regional output.

Forecasts of civilian employment by industry are obtained from forecasts of output by industry using existing sales-employee ratios. Forecasts of the total civilian population are obtained by multiplying total civilian employment by the ratio of civilian population to civilian employment. Total population is obtained by adding estimates of the total military population of the region to forecast civilian population.

Population forecasts for each of the four counties comprising the study area are based on analyses of past trends, combined with ad hoc assumptions regarding the manner in which the region will develop. The two most important of these assumptions are the continuation of the trend toward concentration of population growth in the immediate periphery of existing primary urban centers, and the fact that a number of transportation projects already in progress affect the pattern of development in specified ways.

Employment Allocation Models

The techniques used to allocate industry employment for plans A and B are identical. They differ only in the distribution of industrial sites available. Available sites are defined in this model as vacant land zoned for industrial use and inactive industrial parks. The techniques used to allocate industrial employment were designed to allocate employment only in areas outside the Seattle-Tacoma central business districts (CBDs). Independent estimates of CBD employment were constructed for the study by Larry Smith and Company, a Seattle-based consulting firm with considerable experience in real estate market analysis.

Regional employment minus that of the Seattle and Tacoma CBDs, called the employment residual, was allocated to subzones as follows. First, those industries which, in the regional employment forecast, were not projected to grow were assumed to maintain their 1961 locations. Second, employment in those industries projected to decline was reduced proportionally at the base-year locations of the industries. Finally, a two-tiered procedure was used to allocate employment increments in those projected to expand. Existing firms were surveyed about their employment intentions, and the "intended" future increments to employment were allocated to the site locations of the firms. With these totals subtracted from the employment to be allocated outside the CBDs, a second-stage procedure was used to allocate remaining employment increments to subzones. This method involved matching the locational requirements of growing industries with available sites.

Both the new firms and prospective sites were scored in terms of their need or possession of the following characteristics, all defined qualitatively: freeway proximity, water transportation, railroad facilities, and access to the labor force. Available sites were divided further into two classes according to their desirability, and the overflow of firms from a given zone of better sites was then assigned to lesser location sites.

The methods used to allocate retail employment differed for plan A and plan B projections. Under both plans a separate analysis of the future growth of the retail sales in the area's two main shopping districts, the Seattle and Tacoma CBDs, was conducted by the research staff, using methodology designed by Larry Smith and Company. Among the factors considered in the forecasts of CBD retail sales were the presence of suburban growth and competition. Evaluation of these factors relied heavily on marketing forecasts of local firms, the trend in retail sales by location during the period 1958–61, and estimates of the amount of unused capacity in the CBDs. Working against the full utilization of the Tacoma district were the unfinished Seattle-Tacoma Freeway and a faltering downtown urban renewal project.

Retail goods were divided into convenience and comparison goods. Convenience-goods outlets were defined as food and drug stores, eating and drinking places, and gas stations. Comparison-goods outlets included all other retail establishments.

Comparison-goods employment under plan A was allocated first to the CBDs on the basis of the above considerations. The residual was allocated to suburban areas on the basis of judgment. By contrast, convenience-goods employees were allocated to zones outside of the CBDs using the following two-stage procedure: (1) Employees were first allocated to analysis zones which received a comparison-goods employment change of 1,000 or more, at the ratio (derived from 1961 data) of one convenience-goods employee to four comparison-goods employees; and (2) the remaining amount of district employment change was prorated to zones which did not receive employment in the first step.

Under plan B the basic assumption was made that comparison-goods retail employment follows population at the large-trade-area level. Existing towns in the plan B radial corridors were considered large trade areas. Total comparison-goods employment change for each town was distributed in proportion to the town's total population change. The employment allocated to each town, less the employment increment to the towns currently planned by retailers, was distributed to those analysis zones in the towns that already had an existing or planned comparison center. These increases in the towns' retail employment, under plan B, took place at the expense of suburban areas.

The shift of convenience-goods employment to the towns in plan B resulted solely from shifts in population. This employment was allocated to tracts within the towns by methods nearly identical to those described for plan A.

In allocating office service employment to zones outside the CBDs multiple regression analysis was used. This analysis related the level of office service employment to the level of retail employment, with about 85 per cent of the variation in office service employment explained. The actual allocation was performed using a two-step procedure: (1) Office employment was distributed to zones exhibiting an increased comparison-goods retail employment in centers of 1,000 or more, at the rate of one office employee to every four employees in retail comparison goods (a rate established from 1961 data); and (2) office service employment not yet allocated within the district was prorated to the other zones in the district, one-half according to their 1961 office employment and one-half according to their projected 1985 comparison-goods employment. This rule was developed by trial and error in an attempt to recognize the nucleating effect of present clusters of office activity.

Under plan B the projected office employment for the CBDs was broken down into categories. The locational requirements of each category were then taken into consideration for determining the level of employment for allocation to each CBD. The residual was distributed to subareas on the basis of forecasts of retail trade by subarea.

Population Allocation Models

The spatial allocation of the population residing in large multifamily structures (more than twenty units), hotels, and motels was done on a judgmental basis. The spatial allocation of the population residing in single-family and small multifamily structures (less than twenty units) was obtained by using a series of multiple regression models. The multiple regression models recognized an important complexity of the urban land market—the asymmetrical behavior of older and newer parts of metropolitan areas. To allow for these differences, separate regression models were used in forecasting population change in growing and declining areas.

The forecasting model for growing areas had as its dependent variable the logarithm of the ratio of the actual to the "hypothetical" total population change for a particular zone or subarea. Hypothetical change is that which would result if residential land availability were the only determinant of relative population growth, and the increases in population were allocated in proportion to the amount of land available in the subareas. For example, if a study tract has 10 per cent of the available land in the area, then the hypothetical change would be 10 per cent of the total population change in the entire area. In this population growth model the significant explanatory variables were access to employment, income, and occupation; housing conditions; lot size permitted by zoning; and the size of the land parcel under single control. Employment accessibility was defined as

$$A_i = (S_1/T^x_{i-1}) + (S_2/T^x_{i-2}) + \ldots + (S_n/T^x_{i-n})$$

where A_i is an index of accessibility of zone i to employment in all other zones; S_n is the number of employees in zone n; T_{i-n} is the travel time, including terminal time, between zones i and n; and x is an exponent representing the tripmaker's resistance to distance. The exponent used in the accessibility calculations was 2, based on calibrations made in an earlier study for Washington, D.C.

For analysis zones inside areas that grew between 1950 and 1960, the following steps were taken to distribute future population: (1) Projected values for the independent variables were determined for each analysis zone. (2) These values were substituted into the equation to give, for each of the population growth zones, the logarithm of the ratio of actual to hypothetical growth. (3) The logarithms were transformed into their antilogs and multiplied by the capacity of the available residential land; this produced a growth index for each zone. (4) The control totals for the 1961 to 1985 population change by county were distributed to analysis zones by prorating them according to the size of the computed growth index. (5) The population distribution for each analysis zone was then checked to assure that it did not exceed the holding capacity of the zone; if the distribution did, in fact, exceed holding capacity, excess population was removed, the filled zones were removed from those available, and the fourth step was repeated.

Distribution between the two types of housing (single-family and small multifamily structures) was made holding the base-year proportions constant across the entire area, although variance among the counties was permitted.

The projection model for declining areas was also based on a multiple regression equation. In this instance the percentage decline in population within census tracts was the dependent variable. It was dependent on the occupations and incomes of the inhabitants and the condition of the housing stock. The independent variables were projected and substituted into the equation. The resulting forecast values were then adjusted judgmentally. The total population decline in these declining tracts is the sum of the forecast decline of individual zones.

The population distribution obtained for plan B differs in only minor respects from that in plan A. In making the plan B forecasts, the coefficients of lot size and land availability variables were both increased in the model for forecasting population change in growing areas. This affected the holding capacities of the areas and a shift took place to more land-intensive residences. The procedure was otherwise identical to that used in forecasting the spatial distribution of population for plan A. Both the forecasts of population and employment by zone were then converted to residential and industrial space requirements, using person-per-type-of-housing-space ratios or existing employee-space ratios.

With the exceptions of the space requirements for miscellaneous government, military, and domestic service employment, the above schema outlines the manner in which the land-use allocation was carried out.

OVERVIEW

The Puget Sound study deserves praise for its innovations in the development of land-use models. However, certain shortcomings are also discernible.

One shortcoming concerns the reasoning underlying the projected location of industry. The spatial distribution model for industry relies heavily on the premise that current locations represent equilibrium locations. This premise is incorporated into the assumption that firms located in the region during the base year will not move over the next twenty-five years. Casual observation argues against this assumption, especially in view of the systematic and numerically large movement of certain industries out of central cities. Another weak point is that changes in the transportation system were not incorporated into the industrial location decision.

There are some questions, also, about the procedure for allocating employment to the CBD. To some extent this occurred because the documentation of the methodology is very limited. For example, it is not clear whether the control totals for the CBD projections are consistent with the control totals used in the land-use model. Further, the procedure of determining CBD employment independent of the other parts of the model is somewhat dubious; for example, CBD retail employment is determined independent of residential location.

In terms of the distribution of population, the model does attempt to place shadow prices on locational costs by including characteristics of housing, such as lot size, housing condition, and size of land parcel under individual control. No allowance is made, however, for increased densities in sections of the study area. Because the dependent variable is the log of the ratio of actual to hypothetical population change in a zone, it is not possible for increases in population to occur in those zones in which there is no vacant land. This excludes the possibility of replacing low-density with higher-density dwellings, either through new construction or filtering. This problem is common to models of the housing market where demolition and filtering are neglected.

4

Southeastern Wisconsin Regional
Planning Commission Study

INTRODUCTION

THE SOUTHEASTERN WISCONSIN Regional Planning Commission
(SEWRPC) is an advisory commission charged with the study and
planning of the physical facilities of the region. The regional land-
use–transportation study, initiated in 1963, followed the planning
sequence shown in Figure 4. As can be surmised from this figure,
the Southeastern Wisconsin spatial allocation models are not meant to
be pure forecasting models. Rather, the models are intended to be
part of the planning process. Their role is to test the feasibility of
alternative design plans, identify significant policy variables, and
make explicit the important feedbacks in the system.

The first step in the planning sequence was the projection of regional
employment and population. Two sets of projections were produced
for this purpose, each using a different methodology. The first was a
conventional forecast developed by dividing the regional industries
into dominant and subdominant, and then examining and forecasting
growth of the dominant industries in detail. The Commission also
developed a complex regional economic simulation, which forecasts
employment by categories.[1] The employment forecasts were used to
estimate future population and land-use requirements.

The second step is the development of a land-use plan. The
Southeastern Wisconsin Regional Commission is in the process of

---

[1] The model is an input-output model structured from the work of S. Chakra-
varty, *The Logic of Investment Planning,* Amsterdam, 1959.

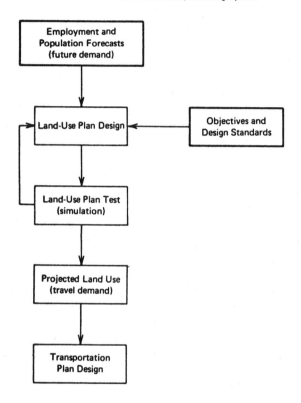

Figure 4
Southeastern Wisconsin
Land-Use — Transportation Study Planning System

Source: Adapted from Southeastern Wisconsin Planning Commission,
Technical Report No. 3.

building a design model that would produce an optimal land-use configuration on the basis of stated land requirements, some broad
objectives, and specified design standards. Work on this model is continuing in anticipation of its use in future planning. Meanwhile, a more
conventionally structured land-use plan has been incorporated into
the actual planning.

The Commission tests the feasibility of any land-use plan by means
of a dynamic land-use simulation model that its staff developed. This
model, which will be discussed in detail later, is intended to simulate

land development within the region. The simulations provide tests of the plan and assist in identifying the control variables that will be required in order to implement the plan. In addition, the model can be used to forecast future land development under alternative policy assumptions. The dynamic feature of this land-use simulation differentiates it sharply from the more traditional single-stage forecasts.

Conventional methods are used to derive trip generation and modal split from land use. This information is used to develop a transportation plan which feeds back on the land-use simulation by altering the access time to both employment and commercial centers. Continued iteration between the transportation plan and the land-use simulation results in a transportation system that satisfies the land-use plan.

METHODOLOGY

The land-use simulation model is dynamic and behavioral. Land is divided into five sectors by use: residential, services, industrial, special, and agricultural. The residential sector is the model's prime mover. The service sector, which includes all land use that is dependent on access to residential or industrial land, simply reacts to changes in residential and industrial location. The industrial sector roughly corresponds to the traditional basic industries. Special land use includes all exogenously introduced nonindustrial land use. It consists mostly of highways, parks, and other government uses. Location of employment in both the industrial and special sectors is taken as exogenous to the model. Agricultural land use is taken as a residual after the other four sectors have been determined.

Residential Land Use

Residential land location is depicted as resulting from three related decisions. Without specifying order or causal relationships, these decisions are: (1) the land developer's decision to develop land for residential use; (2) the housing builder's decision to construct dwelling units on the developed land; (3) the householder's decision to rent or buy the constructed dwelling units.

The model's logic is predicated on the assumption that households determine the number and type of dwelling units, including the lot size, but that the developer decides the site location for new construction. A schema of the model is shown in Figure 5.

Demand for housing in each period comes from newly created households, in-migrating households, and households relocating within the

Figure 5
Synthesized Flow Diagram for the
Southeastern Wisconsin Residential Model

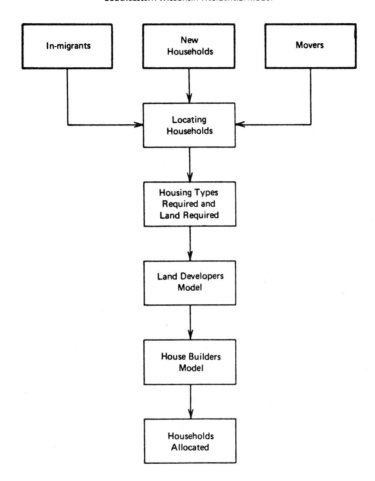

region. The first two groups are given exogenously to the model from the regional economic model. The third is determined endogenously by applying a relocation rate, derived from historical data, to the households in each of the region's zones. Housing supply in each period consists of units vacated by intraregional movers and new construction.

Households are classified into sixteen groups, according to education, occupation, income, age, sex of head, and race. Each of these groups is assigned a relocation rate within the region and a distribution of housing type choices. Regional total demand for housing, by housing type, is obtained and used in the land developer's and builder's decisions about the number and type of lots and housing units to be constructed.

Given the number of lots of each type to be developed within the entire area, a linear programing procedure is used to assign the quantity of development by type to each zone. The model allows five different lot sizes. The cost of developing each lot size varies with type of soil and physical characteristics of the site. Raw land costs are not included in development costs. Development in each period takes place in those zones having the minimum cost of development. The solution given by the linear programing problem minimizes land development costs subject to the constraints that a predetermined number of lots of each size are developed and no more land is developed in each zone than is available, including the land needed by the service sector to support the residential use.

The builder simply constructs houses on the developed land. The quantity of each type of housing to be constructed, in each zone and in each time period, is determined by recursive programing on the basis of actual houses constructed in the past and a given vacancy rate. Finally, the location of the sixteen household groups is determined by matching the available housing types with the choices of each group. In addition to having appropriate housing types, the zone must satisfy an accessibility constraint peculiar to each group. Access is measured in terms of the transportation time to employment, shopping, and population.[2]

---

[2] We have not been able to determine from any of the published material of the Southeastern Wisconsin Regional Planning Commission, or from our correspondence with K. J. Schlager, Chief Systems Engineer of the SEWRPC, the nature of this accessibility constraint or its operational function within the model. An article by Schlager ("A Recursive Programming Theory of the Residential Land Development Process," *Highway Research Record,* 207, 1967) suggests that the accessibility constraint is in fact a "capacity" constraint imposed on the distribution of household types in each zone. The "capacity" in this constraint is the amount and distribution of accessible activities that affect the household location decision. The demand for the capacity of each activity in each zone is the summation of the demand of households to which this activity is accessible, accessibility being a simple binary variable (i.e., capacity is accessible to a household or it is not). However, we have not been able to determine whether this capacity constraint is the accessibility constraint mentioned in published descriptions of the SEWRPC or not.

Industrial Land Use

Two methods are suggested for determining industrial land use in the Southeastern Wisconsin study. It is not clear which method or combination of methods was incorporated in the final model. One method is simply to assign industrial locations consistent with the overall land-use design plan. All output of this model is conditional on an exogenously specified distribution of industrial employment. In practice, this land must be made available to industry by being cleared and provided with requisite services.

The alternative method is to use a linear programing algorithm to determine industrial location. This procedure is similar to that described for allocating residential site land development. Again, the solution is obtained from a linear programing problem to minimize development costs, subject to the constraint that the demand for land must be satisfied. In addition, industries are permitted to locate only in zones having certain characteristics, that is, those that satisfy a number of specific industry constraints.

Service Sector

The quantity of land used by the service sector in each zone is determined by applying a historical ratio of service to residential and industrial land use. The quantity of service land use in each zone, in turn, changes the accessibilities used in the residential location simulation model, and thus affects the location of land development, new construction, and households in the next time period.

Special and Agricultural Sectors

As explained above, the special sector consists mostly of highways, parks, and government offices. The quantity of land in each zone devoted to this sector is determined exogenously. Agricultural land use is simply the residual in each zone after the quantity of land used by the other four sectors is determined.

OVERVIEW

The technique for testing the feasibility of the land-use design by means of land-use simulation models in the Southeastern Wisconsin Regional Land-Use and Transportation Study is unique. This model is distinguished by its attempt to incorporate behavioral aspects into its design. Still, important questions about the comprehensiveness of the model must be raised.

In the "taxonomic analysis" used to classify households in order to match them with housing unit types, one is struck not so much by the variables used as by the absence of variables usually thought to be of major importance in determining households' choices among housing types. These include the size of families, number of automobiles, and number of workers. In addition, in this analysis racial detail seems clearly deficient. Only nonwhite households with female heads were separately analyzed. The model suffers, as do most of this type, from its exclusion of the effect of depreciation or demolition of existing housing structures on decisions to develop previously undeveloped land. Neglect of the importance of the housing stock is particularly striking in a model that is otherwise quite detailed as to housing supply.

While the model has included the behavior of households relocating in order to change their housing bundle, the modeling of movers does not appear to be adequate. For example, each of the household types is assigned a relocation rate and this rate is applied to all zones. One suspects that moving behavior, even by household type, is very dependent on location. Further, it is likely that grouping new households, movers, and in-migrants into the same categories with respect to their demand for new housing may mix some very different behavioral groups.

One of the methods used for determining industrial site locations could be a potential source of trouble. In it, industries have simply been placed where the planners would like them to locate, with the hope that they will somehow be induced to locate on these sites. Given the pivotal importance of industry location in the SEWRPC model, it is very strange that none of the published reports suggest an industry location routine, judgmental or otherwise. The primary function of the model is to simulate the consequence of an industry locational pattern on nonindustrial land use, so that adjustments can be made in controlling parameters (transportation facilities, zoning laws, etc.) to obtain a general land-use configuration that satisfies certain design objectives. It seems highly improbable that the configuration of controls satisfying nonindustrial land-use objectives also suffices to induce industry to locate on planned sites. Clearly, insufficient attention has been given by SEWRPC to the specification of variables and parameters affecting industry location.

5

Atlanta Region Metropolitan Planning Study

INTRODUCTION

THE OBJECTIVE OF the Atlanta area study was to predict the demand for transportation in 1983 and, as an intermediate step, the land use for the area in the same year. The Atlanta model is not a mathematical model, but rather a series of steps employing judgments based on empirical analyses.[1] With models of this form, linkages and feedbacks are not always explicitly stated.

An overview of the Atlanta procedure is given in Figure 6. The model begins with the determination of areawide totals for employment, population, mean family income, and the age distribution of the population. The next step is the allocation of industrial employment within the area. Population is allocated to zones as a function of access to the projected employment locations. On the basis of the population locations and areawide mean family income, mean family income by zone is projected judgmentally.

The increment in the housing stock (types of residences) and changes in housing density are determined on the basis of the population allocation, mean family incomes by zone, and assumptions re-

---

[1] The papers describing the methodology used for the Atlanta study are vague in parts. Consultation with the principal researchers and the consultants to the project, Hammer, Greene, Siler, and Associates, indicates that the vagueness often corresponds to those places where judgmental methods were used the descriptions of which were too lengthy for inclusion in reports. A good deal of time has been used attempting to specify and state explicitly the nature of the judgmental steps.

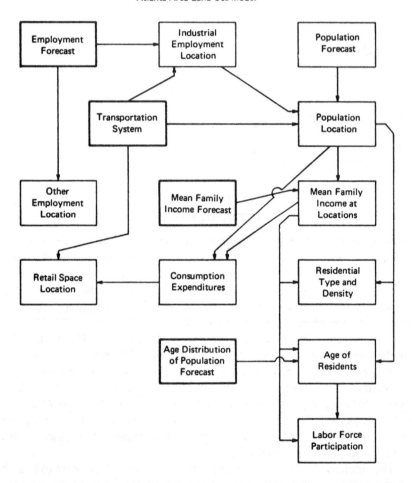

Figure 6
Synthesized Flow Diagram for the
Atlanta Area Land-Use Model

garding the form of new housing construction. Then the age distribution of the population within each zone is determined.

Zonal labor force participation depends upon the age distribution of the population and the mean family income.

Using income and population distributions, the level of total consumption expenditures by zone is ascertained. The allocation of demand to a particular retail location depends on the transportation system and the spatial distribution of demand for retail purchases.

It is this combination of factors, along with several other assumptions, that determines the distribution of retail land use. After the land-use pattern of the area is determined, the transportation requirements of the new spatial form are derived, based on the physical characteristics of the area and the economic and demographic characteristics of its inhabitants.

Allocation by geographic subareas is accomplished in three steps: (1) allocation to intermediate areas composed of one or more census tracts; (2) allocation within the intermediate areas to the census tracts; and (3) allocation to the zones within each census tract. Three types of intermediate areas are defined: built-up areas consisting of those census tracts that are now fully developed and in which it is reasonable to expect a leveling-off or actual decline in population; rural areas consisting of those census tracts that, according to certain criteria, are not recommended for population growth; and expansion areas consisting of those census tracts that should be expected to receive the major impact of future population growth.

METHODOLOGY

Population and Employment Projections

Population projections are based on national projections made by the U.S. Bureau of the Census. It is assumed that the Atlanta area will continue to share in the nation's population growth at the same rate as during the 1950–60 period. Of the four census projections of national population, the one predicting the smallest increase is used. The age distribution of the population is also estimated on the basis of projected national distributions.

Employment levels in the Atlanta area are projected by using two methods, which yield very similar total employment projections. One method bases the projection on an analysis of past trends and estimates of the future potential of various industry groups, for the country and for the Atlanta area. The other method links employment to demographic projections. It predicts future employment by analyzing the sex and age profiles of the projected population and then estimating labor force participation, the resident labor force, unemployment, and multiple jobholders.

Allocation of Industrial Employment

The employment increment in each of thirteen industry groups is assigned to one of four types of employment location. These assignments are based on an analysis of each group's location orientation. The four types of employment locations are central places, industrial districts and parks, population-linked areas, and special areas. Special areas include airports and hospitals; their employment is allocated exogenously. Separate routines are used to allocate those industry groups assumed to be attracted to the first three area types. The routine allocating employment attracted to population-linked areas is described in the retail land-use section of this report.

Employment in those industries attracted to central places and industrial districts and parks is allocated to subareas with an algorithm that ranks industry groups by their preferences, in the base year, for certain locational factors and subareas by their possession of these factors. Employment in each industry group is then allocated to those subareas that most closely satisfy the group's preferences. No method is specified for handling industrial trade-offs or bidding among groups.

Allocation of Population

The first step in the allocation of population is to assign population to built-up rural areas on the basis of current urban renewal plans, planned private projects, probable installation of utility services to outlying areas, and planning staff recommendations. The remaining population is assigned to expansion areas by means of the following formula:

$$p_i = P_t(A_iH_iK_i)/\sum_m(A_mH_mK_m)$$

where p_i is predicted population in tract i, P_t is predicted total population, A_m is accessibility by auto and transit to employment,[2] H_m is tract holding capacity, K_m is an adjustment factor.

Determination of Mean Family Income

The procedure used to estimate the 1983 mean family income by census zone begins by predicting the 1983 mean family income for the Atlanta area. The income prediction is derived from the projected national mean family income by assuming that Atlanta's family income

---

[2] Construction of an access index involved studying various maps to determine accessibility and the presence of various other desirable factors. A maximum value of access of 1.0 was given for the CBD, and values for all other areas used the CBD as a reference. This ranking system was clarified in a conversation with Margaret Breland, Chief of Research, Atlanta Regional Metropolitan Planning Commission, a participant in the study.

will increase slightly, relative to that of the United States. Next, an average for each county in the area is subjectively determined by comparing the 1961 and 1983 family distributions and the 1961 income distribution. Estimates of census tract income are based on the country averages and the socioeconomic characteristics of the population anticipated in the tract, taking into account housing age and quality, land use, racial occupancy, and other relevant factors. The zone incomes are computed by rating each zone within the tract relative to the tract average. The rating is based on anticipated development characteristics.

Housing and Residential Density

Population estimates and the mean family income in each zone, along with some assumptions about the future composition of the housing stock in the region, permit estimation of type of housing units and residential density in each zone. Analysis of data on the Atlanta housing market led to the assumptions that (1) the number of persons per housing unit would decline over the period; (2) housing units in multifamily structures would be about 35 per cent of all new residential construction over the period; (3) housing units in high-rise structures would be about 10 per cent of all new multifamily structures; (4) all new residential construction in the built-up area would be of the multifamily types; and (5) the trend toward a higher proportion of multifamily construction in suburban areas would continue.

The increment of housing units in each zone is obtained by comparing projected and base-year population, then adjusting the stock to meet the increased demand. The normal vacancy rate for new housing is assumed to be 3 per cent. Residential densities, supplied by local planning agencies, are applied to the housing inventory to calculate the increment in net residential acreage.

To review this procedure: Changes in demand are estimated from changes in population between 1961 and 1983 for each zone; the form of the new units is determined by assumptions regarding new construction; total housing stock is obtained by adjusting for average vacancy rates; and, finally, residential acreage for each zone is estimated.

Allocation of the Labor Force

An analysis of the 1961 labor force was undertaken to determine the effect of socioeconomic characteristics on labor force participation rates. The factors tested include the age distribution, mean family income, and racial characteristics of the zones. The age distribution and mean family income were found to have a significant effect on participation rates. The procedure used to determine labor force participation takes account of these factors.

The distribution of the labor force to zones is accomplished in a two-step process. First, the spatial age distribution of the population is projected. Then, on the basis of the age distribution and mean family income for each zone, each zone's labor force is estimated.

The age distribution of the noninstitutional 1983 population for each zone is projected on the basis of assumptions about differential population gains among the counties. The four outer counties are assumed to receive more than proportional increases in the younger age groups. Fulton County is assumed to contain a larger proportion of people over eighteen years of age. A study of the 1961 age distribution in each tract zone yielded sixty-eight age distributions depending on income, race, and housing characteristics. The 1983 zonal age distributions are projected by matching forecast zone characteristics with the sixty-eight age distributions. The most significant change affecting the age distribution between 1961 and 1983 is the spread of multi-family housing to suburban zones.

Labor force participants in the fourteen–nineteen and twenty–sixty-four age groups are distributed to zones in proportion to each zone's share of metropolitan population in the same age classes. This age grouping is made to take account of the higher variance of the four-teen–nineteen-year-old group's participation rates. The sum of the labor force participants for each zone in these two age groups is then adjusted by an income factor. This yields an estimate of the number of labor force participants in each zone.

Retail Land Use

As a last step, the model forecasts space requirements for the retail trade sector and the allocation of this space in the area. Sales totals, instead of employment, are used to compute space requirements. Total area retail sales are estimated from the population and income projections. It is assumed that there will be no change in proportion of retail sales made to nonresidents of the area. The ratio of convenience goods to total expenditure is projected on the basis of the 1958–63 trend.

Retail sales are judgmentally distributed to the five counties within the study area. It is assumed that the CBD's share of retail sales will decline, but that dollar sales will increase at a reasonable rate. Residual sales (i.e., those not allocated to the CBD) are allocated to the outlying counties on the basis of their purchasing power and existing and anticipated retail facilities.

The projected retail sales are converted to total space requirements. A space performance or need level is assigned to each major retail group in each county to estimate overall space additions.[3] The allocation of retail space to tracts and zones is made on a judgmental basis. Location of comparison-goods space involves subjectively locating major regional shopping centers and estimating their overall size. The remaining comparison-goods space is distributed to locations on the basis of major street placements. Convenience-goods store space is distributed on the basis of population changes and certain judgmental factors.

These projections of retail floor space are then converted into sales by tract and zone using sales-space ratios. These ratios are a function of store type—convenience or shopper—and are varied among the tracts in an unspecified manner.

OVERVIEW

Clearly it is questionable to view the distribution of population and the assignment of housing type as a sequential rather than a simultaneous process. It can be strongly argued that the two decisions are not independent. For example, a family might prefer to live considerably nearer to the city if it is to live in a multifamily dwelling.

The model does make some provision for increasing densities in built-up areas by assuming construction of only multifamily structures in these zones. It does not, by contrast, formally consider the effects of filtering and demolition on the housing stock.

In determining the location of industry, the Atlanta model considers the locational characteristics of all—rather than only the recently moving—firms. As will be discussed more extensively in Chapter 9, this method introduces biases that tend to perpetuate the historical locational pattern.

[3] The space performance level refers to the sales-land ratio, which depends on operational characteristics (i.e., the degree of self-service sales in the establishment) and other factors causing space to be more efficiently utilized. These were projected by the consultants to the projects.

Atlanta's heavy reliance on judgments also suggests possible difficulties. These judgments may result in forecasts of land use that are quite good, given present information. In a continuing planning program, however, it is very important to introduce new information over time. Without careful specification of the basis for judgment (a difficult and rarely accomplished task) it is not clear how new information can be introduced or properly used. The problem of incorporating new information is exacerbated as new personnel, unfamiliar with the informal judgment bases of the model, join the planning staff. In short, a more formal and more specified procedure would facilitate the incorporation of new people and new information into the planning process.

6

Detroit Regional Transportation and Land-Use Study

INTRODUCTION

THE DETROIT REGIONAL Transportation and Land-Use Study (TALUS) is a four-year project intended to provide estimates of growth and development in the Detroit area through the year 1990. The purposes of the models and analytical procedures are to estimate the change in land use and in socioeconomic and demographic characteristics of the zones in the region. These models were developed cooperatively by CONSAD Research Corporation and the TALUS staff.

As part of these efforts, a Southeastern Michigan growth model (SEMOD) was developed; a schema of it is presented in Figure 7. For this model, the Detroit area is broken into 297 districts, each of which is further divided into zones (1,446 total). The model requires exogenous forecasts of the area's employment by industrial groups, total households by income class and life cycle, and total population by age and sex cohort. The model then forecasts employment in nine employment groups for each of the districts. These forecasts are made on the basis of characteristics (e.g., lagged employment, households, access) of the districts. The household-income models first forecast changes in total households by district, then changes in the number of households in each of seven income classes. The final step is the forecast of total households and households by income class for each zone. At each stage in the household-income model the new forecasts are adjusted to the control totals for the previous stage.

A separate model forecasts the number of households by life cycle

Figure 7
Synthesized Flow Diagram for the
Southeastern Michigan Growth Model

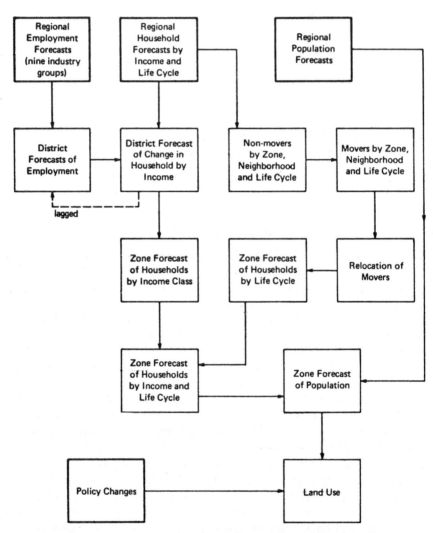

for each zone, first forecasting nonmoving households. By subtracting this estimate from total households by life cycle in each zone, the model generates a group of moving households originating from each zone broken down by life cycle. These movers are allocated to destination zones on the basis of their origin zone, life cycle, and the characteristics of available zones. The total number of households by life cycle in each zone after movers are allocated is the sum of non-movers and new locators, and this total is reconciled with the previous forecast of households by zone.

Total population is forecast using a relationship between households by life cycle and population, estimated with 1965 data. Forecasting land use by zone is essentially a bookkeeping task, given previously specified commercial, industrial, public, and semipublic land use and new residential requirements.

The model also forecasts car ownership and recreation participation, but these are not shown in Figure 7, nor will they be discussed, since they are not directly a part of the subject matter of this review.

METHODOLOGY

Population and Employment Control Totals

The aggregate population and employment forecasts are essentially expansions of a Michigan manpower study. Greater detail is developed, however, for the Detroit area. Shift and share analysis techniques are employed, as well as an input-output analysis for the region. The final estimate is described as a forecast "demand for labor," and a conversion is made to obtain the labor supply in categories such as age, sex, and education level. Population totals are derived from these labor supply estimates.

Employment Model

Separate equations for each of nine employment sectors[1] are used to estimate employment for each district. Calibration of these equations is based on 1953 data for districts.[2] The equations are estimated using linear regression techniques. While each of the nine equations is slightly different, they can be broadly described as forecasting district employment as a function of that industry's lagged employment, some other industries' lagged employment, dummy variables relating to transpor-

---

[1] Transportation equipment manufacturing, other manufacturing, transportation communication and utility, wholesale, retail, F.I.R.E., business and personnel services, professional and related services, and public administration.

[2] Adjustments in the estimated coefficients were necessary because (1) the calibration area was smaller than the prediction area and (2) the model was run over a shorter period than that for which the equations were estimated. These adjustments are explained in the major report.

tation access, and lagged households and income in the district. The model also includes unique adjustments for retail trade in eight districts and for the automotive manufacturing industry in seven districts.

Household-Income Model

In this model regional households are distributed by income class among zones. This is done in two steps: allocation to districts within the region and allocation to zones within each district. The first stage estimates the change in total households and the number of households in each of the nine classes for each district. The predictions of change are made with regression analysis where the dependent variable is the observed changes between 1953 and 1965. The explanatory variables are, broadly speaking, the lagged total number of households, access to employment (employment is sometimes broken into various groups —not necessarily mutually exclusive), change in employment in the district, base-period residential holding capacity, and proportion of land devoted to commercial use. The estimates of these equations are adjusted in light of the total regional forecast of households.

For the highest income class, the explained variance using the above method was found to be unsatisfactory. As a result, the district net change in households with incomes over $15,000 is obtained by estimating the number of these households in each zone and summing for the district totals.

The explanatory variables used to predict the number of households (total and by income class) in a zone are, broadly, the lagged number of households (often by income class), the characteristics of the zone (e.g., proportion of zone in forest, total shoreline, density of residential development), and density constraints set by policy for new development. These forecasts are adjusted to eliminate any negative forecasts and make the zonal total consistent with the district forecasts.

Life-Cycle Model

The life-cycle model allocates households to zones by a family's life style. The distribution of households to zones accomplished by this model is independent of the household forecasts of the household-income model and so the two forecasts must be reconciled. The life cycle model gives some suggestion of being an intrametropolitan moving model, but in fact the model generates movers only as a residual.

Eight neighborhood types are identified, using discriminant and factor analysis on zone characteristics in 1953 and 1965. The zone characteristics used are the proportion of households in each life cycle, the proportion of households in each income class, a few measures of density, and two physical characteristics (proportion of zone in forest and total shoreline). Zones are classified as one of the eight neighborhood types by applying to each the coefficients of the eight sets of factor loadings and by defining the zone to be in the neighborhood class giving the highest score. Zones can be reclassified after each step to reflect policy changes and new state variables forecast.

There are seven life cycle categories. They were defined on an a priori basis in the following categories:

Life Cycle 1: The head of household is unmarried, less than forty-five years of age, and no children are present.

Life Cycle 2: The head of household is married, less than forty-five years of age, and no children are present.

Life Cycle 3: The head of household is married, and the youngest child present is less than five years old.

Life Cycle 4: The head of household is married, and the youngest child is between five and seventeen years of age.

Life Cycle 5: The head of household is married, and the youngest child present is eighteen years old or older.

Life Cycle 6: The head of household is married, forty-five years of age or older, and no children are present.

Life Cycle 7: The head of household is unmarried, forty-five years of age or older, and no children are present.

The model begins by generating nonmovers for each zone. Nonmovers are estimated by life cycle and neighborhood of residence. The explanatory variables in each case are the number of households in the base period in a zone in each life cycle class. Movers for each life cycle and neighborhood are determined by subtracting estimates of nonmoving households from the base-year totals. Total movers by life cycle and previous neighborhood type are obtained by summing over all zones.

These fifty-six values (eight neighborhoods and seven life cycles) are multiplied by a transition matrix giving the probability by life cycle of moving from neighborhood type i to neighborhood j. These movers are then summarized by life cycle and neighborhood of destination. Allocation to particular zones is accomplished by using an attractiveness index calculated for all zones. The attractiveness index gives the proportion of all movers in each life cycle class and from each neighborhood type who will locate in a zone. The attractiveness is measured by the number of households by life cycle and neighborhood who have been in present residence less than five years. The explanatory variables are the number of households by life cycle located in the zone, the zone's relative share of the district's total households in that life cycle, and the zone's residual holding capacity. As explained, the new totals of households, nonmovers plus relocators, must be reconciled with the household-income forecasts.

Population Model

Population is forecast using equations estimated from 1965 data. Separate estimates are made for white and nonwhite populations. The independent variables are, in both cases, the total households in some of the life cycle classes.[3] The forecast equations are:

$$P_{wi} = 267.0 - 5.0 \, LC1_i + 4.6 \, LC3_i + 4.2 \, LC4_i + 3.3 \, LC6_i$$

$$P_{ni} = 0.8 + 2.4 \, LC1_i + 4.4 \, LC3_i + 4.1 \, LC4_i + 3.1 \, LC5_i$$
$$+ 1.3 \, LC6_i + 1.7 \, LC7_i$$

where P_{wi} is white population in zone i, P_{ni} is nonwhite population in zone i, and LCk_i is number of households in life cycle k in zone i.

Land-Use Model

The land-use estimates are largely a bookkeeping situation in which the major force of change consists in exogenously introduced policy decisions. Additions to residential land use, however, are endogenous to the model. Since the model does not allow structures to be torn down or converted to other uses, negative changes can be introduced only exogenously. Vacant and agricultural land use is changed by policy updating.

OVERVIEW

In many ways, the TALUS effort is an important step forward in urban land-use modeling. For example, the attempt to understand changing household locations through an analysis of life cycle and intra-metropolitan migration is highly innovative. Furthermore, the overall plan of the model is quite reasonable and builds well on the best in previous modeling efforts.

---

[3] It is not clear why some average household size by income, life cycle, and neighborhood was not used to estimate population in light of the statistical problem of the multicollinearity among the number of households by life cycle in a zone.

Nevertheless, certain problems remain. For example, the two separate methods for determining allocation of households seem rather artificial. It is also true that, while parts of the model reflect the stated purpose of focusing on changes taking place within the region, there are many areas where the model does not really address change. Totals instead of changes are forecast in the employment allocation model, the household-income model at the zonal level, and the life cycle moving model. The reliance on totals is sometimes required by data limitations, but this is not always the case. For example, employment data were available for both 1953 and 1965.

The model's equations seem to have been determined mainly with regard to maximizing the explained variance. For example, instead of attempting estimates of movers, the model estimates nonmovers. It is quite clear that single equation regression analysis will explain a great deal more of the variance of nonmovers by zone than movers, but this does not imply any better forecast of movers. In essence, the approach taken does not provide more information about what determines moving—which is of greatest interest. It is also difficult to rationalize some of the variables included or the signs of the coefficients. For example, it is difficult to explain why access to a trunk line highway is part of the equation estimating "professional and related services," but not included in the equations for "other manufacturing." Nor is it easy to understand why the change in a district's households in the $3,000 to $6,000 income class is (1) positively related to access to group two employment (transportation, manufacturing, other manufacturing, retail, service, professional, and related); and (2) negatively related to the change in group two employment; or (3) negatively related to access to Group Three employment (which contains transportation manufacturing, other manufacturing, and retail from Group Two, as well as transportation, utilities, and commercial and public administration); and (4) positively related to change in Group Three employment.

7

Bay Area Simulation Study

INTRODUCTION

THE BASS MODEL under review was initiated at the Center for Real Estate and Urban Economics, University of California, Berkeley in 1962. Some of the goals of this study—"analysis of the probable impact of changes in employment on future land uses in the San Francisco Bay Area" and "analysis of the impact of major transportation investment on the structure and distribution of urban land uses in the San Francisco Bay Area"[1]—led to the construction of models similar to those constructed for the Bay Area Transportation Study. Discussions of both the BASS and BATS models are included here in order to illustrate two attempts at a land-use model for the same area (the discussion of the BATS model follows in Chapter 8).

In the BASS model, two employment submodels and one population submodel generate the overall area projections of employment and population for five-year iterations projecting to the year 2020. The two employment forecasts are averaged to get labor demand, which is then compared with labor supply generated by the population model. Demand and supply are reconciled, and employment forecasts for the twenty-one industry groups, as well as a population forecast for the year 2020, are obtained for the thirteen-county Bay Area.

BASS differentiates between the locational determinants of different groups of industries, making use of six different employment location submodels. The employment forecasts are inputs to the employment location submodels.

[1] Institute of Urban Regional Development, *Jobs, People and Land: Bay Area Simulation Study Special Report,* 6, Berkeley, 1968.

A residential location submodel reconciles housing supply and usable land with the housing demand generated by the population forecasts. The submodel uses six housing unit groups based on two structure types (single-family and multifamily) and three values (high, medium, and low). The submodel incorporates approximations of housing filtering and demolition.

Employment locations, with the exception of those for educational services, construction, and agriculture, are determined prior to residential locations. The assumption implicit in this sequence is that retail employment adjusts to the population distribution, both homesite and worksite, that existed at the beginning of a five-year period, while residential location adjusts to changes in the distribution of employment during that period.

METHODOLOGY

The methods for locating employment for the six industry classifications are described briefly as follows:

1. Retail employment—allocated with a combination of a gravity potential model and an attractiveness measure derived from regression analysis.

2. Manufacturing, trucking and warehousing, and wholesaling— allocated by means of an attractiveness measure derived for subareas.

3. Finance, insurance and real estate, education and government— allocated to counties and important subareas of counties on the basis of a simple extrapolation of historical trends, modified judgmentally; residual allocated to other subareas on the basis of population.

4. Services—assigned with a regression model in which employment is a function of density and accessibility.

5. Construction—allocated to subareas as a function of the amount of their new employment and new housing.

6. Agriculture, mining, transportation, communication, and military—total employment from the projection model is allocated to the subareas in the same proportion as at present.

The first four of these models will be discussed in greater detail below; the last two are self-explanatory. Construction is assumed to be related to new housing and new employment, and allocated to subareas on the basis of the proportion of these two activities now being undertaken. The level of agricultural activity is a residual, and agricultural employment is reduced in each subarea in proportion to the removal of agricultural land from the subarea.

Retail Trade

The proportion of new retail trade employment locating in any tract, j, is a function of the percentage of the region's new employment locating in j, the percentage of the area's total population in j, and the relative attractiveness of j. The equation is written as:

$$ALLOC_j^r = \frac{[(\alpha NE_j/\sum_j NE_j) + (\beta POP_j/\sum_j POP_j) + RAI_j]}{2} \Delta EMP^r$$

where $ALLOC_j^r$ is new retail employment in j, NE_j is total new employment in j, POP_j is total population in j, RAI_j is relative attractiveness index of j, ΔEMP^r is areawide new retail employment, and α, β are exogenous constants summing to 1.

Of the above, only RAI needs further explanation. The RAI is a function of the potential demand for retail trade in the tract and the tract's commercial site suitability. Potential demand is the difference between actual demand (employees) already in the tract and expected demand. Expected demand is determined by a gravity model. Commercial site suitability is obtained from a regression equation relating the amount of retail employment to population accessibility, commercial accessibility, industrial accessibility, tract density, and the amounts and location of other types of employment. The two measures are combined as follows:[2]

$$RAI_j = \sqrt{DP_j} \, [1 + 0.5(CSS_j/ \sum_k CSS_k)]$$
$$\div \sum_i \sqrt{DP_i} \, [1 + 0.5(CSS_i/ \sum_k CSS_k)]$$

where DP_j is potential demand and CSS_j is commercial site suitability.

Industrial Land-Use Model: Manufacturing, Trucking and Warehousing, Wholesale Trade

Increases in employment are spatially located by means of weighted indexes of tract locational factors calculated separately for eleven industry groupings. The tract with the highest score for one industrial

[2] The square root and 0.5 were introduced to make the model fit the data better. The form of this function, and many others in the BASS model, is entirely judgmental. There is no attempt to justify it other than to say that it fits the data. These equations are identities and are not estimated.

group receives one average size firm of that industrial group. If more employees are to be located, the indexes are recalculated, taking into account changes from the first allocation. Again, the tract with the highest score receives one firm. This process continues until all employment is located. Allocated employment is converted into land use by means of land absorption coefficients.

The tract scores (S_j^k) are calculated as follows:

$$S_j^k = \sum_i W_i^k I_j^i$$

where k is the industrial group number, j denotes tracts, i is location factors important to industrial group k, S_j^k is the tract score for industry group k, W_i^k is the weight of the i factor for group k, and I_j^i is index of factor i for tract j.

Regression analysis was used to determine weights for the ith factors for each of the eleven employment groups. Among the variables considered were the location of the other industrial firms in the area, rail access, freeway access, vacant land, restaurants, libraries, and tract density. "Industrial location experts" altered the weights judgmentally when they thought it necessary. An index for the ith factor in tract j is calculated by means of the following:

$$I_j^i = (X_j^i - MIN^i)/(MAX^i - MIN^i)$$

where $I_j^i =$ index for factor i in tract j, $X_j^i =$ actual magnitude of the i factor for subarea j, $MIN^i =$ minimum value of X for all j, and MAX^i $=$ maximum value of X for all j.

In the BASS model intra-area industrial migration is recognized and incorporated into the model. The rate at which employment migrates from a tract is a function of the density of the tract. Density is defined as the sum of population and employment per acre. If the density of a tract is greater than ten, some industry migrates from the area. For example, on the basis of historical data, if density per acre is thirty or greater, 10 per cent of all industrial employment in the tract migrates; if density per acre is twenty, then 5 per cent migrates. Migrating employees are added to the pool of new employees to be allocated for each industry. Land released by migration is added to the stock of vacant land in that tract.

When an areawide decline in employment in some industrial group is projected, a different technique is used to determine where employment should be decreased. Instead of reversing the procedure used for growing industries (i.e., decreasing employment in those tracts with the lowest score), BASS introduces a new procedure. The percentage of an industry's total decline to be allocated to each tract is calculated by

$$PLDECL_j{}^k = (EMP_j{}^k \times DEN_j{}^{\frac{1}{2}}) \div \sum{}_m (EMP_m{}^k \times DEN_m{}^{\frac{1}{2}}).$$

The number of employees lost from tract j is determined by

$$EMPLOS_j{}^k = PLDECL_j{}^k \cdot (1.2 \; \Delta EMP^k)$$

where $EMPLOS_j{}^k$ is number of employees of type k lost in tract j, $PLDECL_j{}^k$ is percentage decline in industry k in tract j, is ΔEMP^k is projected decline in employees of type k, DEN is density.

It is clear that $\Sigma_j \; EMPLOS_j{}^k$ will be 120 per cent of the areawide decline of industry k projected in the regional economic projections. BASS allocates an amount equal to this excess decline of 20 per cent by using the growing industry algorithm. This approach to industry decline is introduced in order to take account of the fact that industry decline is a complex occurrence, involving intraregional migration of employment in declining industries.

Finance, Insurance and Real Estate, Education and Government

The geographical breakdown for this locational algorithm is (1) counties, (2) important subareas of counties, and (3) residual subareas. F.I.R.E. and government employment are allocated to counties according to the present proportions, with judgmental modifications. This same combination of history and judgment is used to allocate employment to important subareas within counties. Remaining employment is distributed to the other subareas on the basis of population.

Services

Service employment location is determined in a manner similar to that used for retail employment. Employment is distributed to tracts as a function of a relative attractiveness index and population. The allocating formula is

$$ALLOC_j{}^s = \left(\alpha RAI_j + \beta \frac{POP_j}{\sum{}_i POP_i} \right) \Delta EMP^s$$

where $ALLOC_j{}^s$ is new service employment located in tract j, RAI_j is relative attractiveness index, POP_j is population in tract j, ΔEMP^s is new service employment in area, and α, β are exogenous constants summing to 1.

The RAI is obtained from an equation determined by regression analysis. Different *RAI* equations, including different independent variables, are estimated for (1) eating, drinking and lodging services, (2) personal services, (3) miscellaneous services, and (4) medical and other health services.

Residential Housing Location

The residential allocation simulation can be viewed as a step toward an explicit replication of the housing market. The model separates the treatment of supply and demand. On the supply side the BASS model introduces important but often neglected aspects of the market. These innovations include both housing demolition and filtering.

An exogenously determined overall rate of demolition of existing housing is assumed for the whole area. On the basis of the findings of other independent studies and some BASS investigations of the demolition rate in San Francisco in recent years, demolition is assumed to be 4 per cent of the existing housing per five years. The rate of demolition is not constant for all types of houses. Bureau of Census data show that, in California, demolitions in the sixties could be distributed among housing types in the following ratios:

	High Value	Medium Value	Low Value
Single-family type	1	2	4
Multifamily type	2	4	8

Demolitions in the first five-year period are distributed among the housing types in the assumed ratios, that is, demolitions of low-value multifamily dwellings are eight times those of high-value single-family dwellings. However, because multiple family units have changed in nature from subdivided single-family units and low-quality post-World War II construction to more durable and high-rise types, the rates of demolition of multifamily units are adjusted down 10 per cent in each succeeding period.

The distribution of the demolitions depends on the value of the tract's housing units, the portion of its units representing the multifamily type, and the density of tract development. For single-family dwellings, the tract's proportion of new demolitions is determined as follows:

$$DR_j{}^s = (DD_j)^{\frac{1}{4}} \cdot (PM_j{}^{\frac{1}{2}}/HV_j)$$

where $DR_j{}^s$ is proportion of single-family unit demolition in tract j, DD_j is density of development in tract j, PM_j denotes multiple units as percentage of total housing in tract j, and HV_j is housing values in j, or $(2 \cdot \text{high value} + \text{middle value})/\text{total housing units}$.

A tract's share of multifamly unit demolition depends on the single-family proportion:

$$DR_j{}^m = (DR_j{}^s)^{\frac{1}{2}}.$$

Demolition affects both supply (by changing the number of houses available) and demand (by altering the number of households looking for housing). The effect on housing demand will be considered below.

Filtering of the housing stock does not alter the number of housing units available, but it does change their value distribution. The model assumes that, in each time period, 20 per cent of all high-value housing becomes medium value-housing and 20 per cent of all medium-value becomes low-value housing. No distinction is made here between single-family and multifamily housing units. The conversion of single-family housing units to multifamily units is assumed negligible.

The rate of filtering differs between tracts. The filtering rate on single-family units in tract j depends on the percentage of multifamily units in j and the value of housing in j:

$$FIL_j{}^k = S^k(PM_j{}^{\frac{1}{2}} \cdot HV_j)(H_j{}^k)$$

where $FIL_j{}^k$ denotes net units filtered from housing of type k in j, S^k is scalar factor for housing of type k, PM_j is per cent of multifamily units in j, HV_j is housing values in j, or $(2 \cdot \text{high value} + \text{middle value})/\text{total housing units}$, and H^k_j is number of housing units of type k in j. The rate of multifamily unit filtering in a tract depends only on housing values:

$$FIL_j{}^k = S^k(1/HV_j)(H_j{}^k).$$

The total potential supply of new housing construction in a tract depends on the land supply, slope of the land, attractiveness, housing value distribution, proportion of single-family units, and density. Land supply is the sum of agricultural acreage, usable vacant land, and land freed by migration and demolition. Tract density is defined as the average of the density (defined above) of the tract and of the surrounding tracts.

Potential new housing construction is partitioned into potential single-family and multifamily units, and then into high-value, medium-value, and low-value units. The first partition is made by averaging two ratios: the present percentage of single-family units and the potential percentage. The potential percentage is determined by the density of development in the tract. The second partition depends on three proportions: existing value partition, the density of development, and the slope of the land. The land absorption coefficients used to determine the number of potential new housing units vary with housing type and housing value, and between tracts.

The total demand for new housing is the sum of families forced to move because of demolition and the increase in families projected by the population projection model. The demand is judgmentally partitioned into housing type; a secular decline in the proportion of single-family units is assumed. The proportion of demand for each of the three value classes for single-family units is assumed to be as follows: 36 per cent, high value units; 52 per cent, medium value units; and 12 per cent, low value units. For multifamily units, it is 19 per cent, 51 per cent, and 31 per cent, respectively.

The last step in the residential allocation model is the determination of the location of new housing construction. The proportion of potential new housing construction developed in a tract depends on access to employment.

OVERVIEW

The most interesting innovation in the Bay Area Simulation Study is the introduction of filtering and demolition into the model of the residential housing market. It is commonplace to observe that changes in the stock of housing have major implications for urban form, yet these changes usually are omitted from urban models. BASS makes no attempt to model the behavior behind filtering and demolition but does attempt to simulate the results.

BASS allocates households on the basis of overall access to employment. An alternative approach is to allocate employees of a particular worksite on the basis of access to that worksite. This second methodology is used by the Bay Area Transportation Study. Differences in the resulting population distribution estimates could be very interesting.

The most disturbing feature of BASS is the repeated use of arbitrary equations for allocating employment and households. These equations are not estimated via statistical techniques, but are defined judgmentally. The reason for the particular form (e.g., square root) is never clear. Nor is it clear how significant the resultant relationships are. While this methodology can give good predictions, it probably adds very little to an understanding of the behavioral determinants of the spatial form of urban areas.

8

Bay Area Transportation Study

INTRODUCTION

THE BAY AREA Transportation Study Commission has undertaken a three-part study of alternative land-use–transportation plans for the Bay Area. The first phase is an extensive inventory of employment, population, land use, and traffic patterns. The second stage involves model development for the evaluation of a wide range of alternative land uses and transportation networks. The objective of the second stage is to limit the choices to a small number of feasible alternatives. In a final or third stage these alternatives will be evaluated in much greater detail. The final stage allocation models will generate a more complex set of outputs, which will permit a more detailed and disaggregated transportation network evaluation.

BATS recognizes three allocation problems: location of basic employment, location of population-serving employment, and location of households. The first allocation is handled by a Base Employment Allocation Model (BEMOD). The second and third problems are handled in a Projective Land-Use Model (PLUM). PLUM requires the output of BEMOD (i.e., the location of all base employment) to locate population-serving employment and households. The general structure of the model is shown in Figure 8. At this time, neither BEMOD nor PLUM has been completed, but enough privileged material has been received from William Goldner, Research Director of BATSC, to describe its present structure in substantial detail.

METHODOLOGY

Industry Location

Employment is considered population-serving if its spatial location is determined by the spatial location of households, purchasing power,

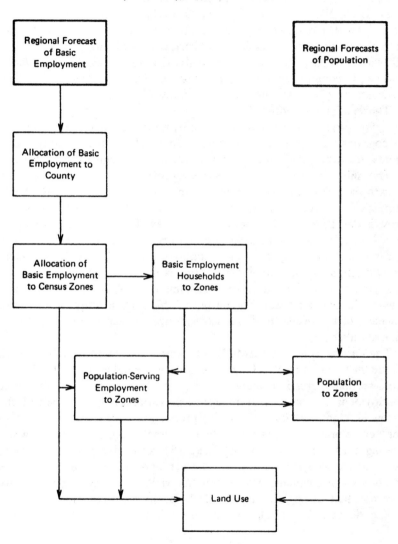

Figure 8
Synthesized Flow Diagram for the
Bay Area Transportation Land-Use Model

and daytime population concentrations. By contrast, employment is basic if its spatial location is determined by interregional transportation routes, resources and unique features, interindustry linkages, and agglomeration economies. While this distinction is not without difficulties, BATSC feels it is a useful dichotomy for modeling spatial allocation.

In BEMOD, basic employment is divided among eight industry groups (with manufacturing further divided into five subgroups): (1) manufacturing (new technology industries, central office, intermediate, fabricated metals, etc., petro-chemical); (2) transportation; (3) wholesaling; (4) communication; (5) business services; (6) state and federal government; (7) agriculture; and (8) mining.

The spatial allocation of each of these industry groups involves a two-step process. First, industry employment increments are allocated to counties using a shift and share model. Then, these county increments are distributed among census tracts using regression analysis.

The shift and share model requires projections of the employment growth of each of the basic industries for the Bay region. BEMOD uses regression analysis on 1950–65 data to estimate the industries' growth deviations in the county from areawide growth. The independent variables in this analysis are density, a lagged rate of growth, intraregional access, and, in some industry groups, lagged employment. In addition, a special judgmental routine is used to allocate unique location employment. Examples of these unique locators are colleges and universities and air fields. The output of this stage is employment totals for each of the twelve basic industry groups in each of the Bay Area's nine counties.

The second stage of BEMOD allocates these county totals to each of the 742 census tracts of the nine-county area. The routine relies on cross-section regression analysis, using 1964 data. Each of the basic employment groups uses as independent variables some subset of the following eight variables: (1) slope, proportion of tract land area, 0–5 per cent slope; (2) mean elevation of tract; (3) presence of water frontage; (4) presence of rail line; (5) accessibility to population, 1965; (6) employment density; (7) tract land use; and (8) tract share of county employment. The β weights yielded by the regression are held constant throughout the 1968–90 projection period.

The dependent variable in this regression is

$$Z_{ij} = (E_{ij}/L_j)/(E_{ik}/L_k)$$

where i is basic industry class, j is census tract, k is county, E is employment, and L is total land occupied by basic industry. The projected value of Z is then substituted into the following equation:

$$\Delta E_{ij}{}^{t+1} = Z^*{}_{ij}\,\Delta E_{ik}{}^{t+1}\,(L_j{}^t/L_k{}^t)$$

where $Z^*{}_{ij}$ is the estimated value. Tract employment is given by

$$E_{ij}{}^{t+1} = E_{ij}{}^t + \Delta E_{ij}{}^{t+1}$$

where the superscript, t, indicates a time period.

The land absorption coefficients used to convert incremental employment to incremental land requirements are tract specific. If incremental land demanded is less than the land available in a tract, BEMOD simply updates the employment land use and proceeds. If the increment is greater, the employment change of the industry with the lowest Z_{ij} is removed from the tract and is allocated to other tracts where land is available.

Population-serving Employment and Households (PLUM)

Both population-serving employment and household locations are determined by PLUM, which uses both the employment projections and the base employment locations. Further, PLUM makes use of exogenous information from local planning agencies—for example, information on preemption of land by government agencies, important for determining the upper limit on the quantity of land available.

The basic idea behind all of PLUM's allocations is that there is some function which gives the probability that an individual working in i will live t minutes from i or will shop in a store t minutes from i. The distribution function decided upon in all cases is of the following form:

$$P_t = e^{\alpha - \beta/t}$$

where P_t is the probability of an individual living less than t from his place of employment. In order to determine the probability for some interval t to $(t+k)$, it is necessary to evaluate the difference between the cumulative probability at $(t+k)$ and t. Formally, this is

$$P_{(t,\ t+k)} = P_{t+k} - P_t = e^{\alpha - \beta/(t+k)} - e^{\alpha - \beta/t}$$

where $P_{(t,\ t+k)}$ is the probability of an individual living in the interval t to $(t+k)$.

These functions are fitted separately for each of the nine counties with data from home interviews. The functions were estimated separately for home to work, home to shop, and work to shop. The estimated functions for counties are then applied to the county's zones to derive three matrices of probabilities for each of the trips to every zone.

In order to locate population-serving employment, PLUM makes use of a variant on the base multiplier technique. Instead of relating population-serving employment to base employment, PLUM relates it to base population, that is, base employment plus families of base employees. PLUM gets the latter by distributing base employees to residential zones by means of the home-to-work probability distribution matrix, P_5, and then applying the historical ratio of the nonworking population of each of the zones.

Formally, these two steps are

$$r_1 = P_5 e_1$$

where r_1 is the vector of residences of base employees by zone, P_5 is the matrix of work-to-home probabilities by zones, and e_1 is the vector of base employees by zone; and

$$q_1 = (L - I)r_1$$

where q_1 is nonworking base employment population, L is the diagonal matrix of population per employee by zone, and I is the unit diagonal matrix. The multiplier is then determined as:

$$K = E_3/(1e_1 + 1q_1)$$

where K is base multiplier, E_3 is total nonbase employment in area (exogenously supplied), $1e_1$ is total base employment, $1q_1$ is total nonworking base-related population, and 1 is the unit vector.

Applying the base multiplier to nonworking base-related population at zone of residence and base employment at zone of employment generates demand for population-serving employment by zones:

$$d_{4.1} = Kq_1$$
$$d_{2.1} = Ke_1$$

where $d_{4.1}$ denotes the vector of demand by zones for population-serving nonworking base-related population, and $d_{2.1}$ is the vector of demand by zones for population-serving employment-serving base employment at place of work. It is assumed that the same multiplier generates both home-based and work-based demand.

The next step is to locate population-serving employment by zones. This is done by multiplying the two vectors of demand for population-serving employment by the zonal probability matrix for home to shop and work to shop. As described above, each of these probability matrices is derived from separate allocation functions. The calculations are shown as follows:

$$e_{4.1} = P_4 d_{4.1}$$

$$e_{2.1} = P_2 d_{2.1}$$

where $e_{4.1}$ is the vector of population-serving employment serving non-working base-related population, $e_{2.1}$ denotes vector of population-serving employment serving base employment, P_4 is the matrix of home-to-shop probabilities, and P_2 is the matrix of work-to-shop probabilities.

Finally, total population-serving employment by zones is obtained by summing work-based and home-based employment

$$e_3 = e_{4.1} + e_{2.1}$$

where e_3 is total population-serving employment. These values are reconciled, zone by zone, to the areawide projection supplied exogenously to PLUM:

$$C(1) = E_3 / 1 e_3$$

$$e_3' = C(1) e_3$$

where $1e_3$ is the sum of the vector of population-serving employment, and e_3' is the adjusted vector of population-serving employment.

The vector of total employment at place of work is obtained by adding the adjusted population-serving employment to the exogenously determined base employment:

$$e_6 = e_1 + e_3'$$

where e_6 is the vector of total employment at place of work.

Given total employment at place of work, it is now possible to re-apply the home-to-work probability matrix, P_5, and determine workers by place of residence, r_6. By applying the population-per-worker ratio for each zone, L, it is possible to determine the total nonworking population, q_6, by place of residence. These operations are shown below:

$$r_6 = P_5 e_6$$

$$q_6 = (L - I) r_6.$$

It is then necessary to reconcile this total nonworking population with that given exogenously to the model. The correction factor is applied to each zone's nonworking population, and the adjusted nonworking population is added to workers by place of residence to determine the total population for the zones. These steps are summarized as:

$$C(2) = \frac{Q_6}{1q_6}$$

where Q_6 is exogenously determined total area nonworking population, and $1q_6$ is sum over zones of nonworking population.

$$q_6' = C(2)q_6$$

where q_6' is the adjusted vector of nonworking population.

$$n_6' = r_6 + q_6'$$

where n_6' is the adjusted vector of total population.

A change in the population in each zone with no change in the number of workers suggests a change in the population per worker, L. Further, assuming a constant family size, the above changes would suggest a change in the workers per household, F. It is this latter adjusted value that is used to calculate the number of households in each zone

$$h = Fr_6$$

where h is the vector of households in each zone, r_6 is the vector of base employees by place of residence, and F is the diagonal matrix of households per base employee.

With base employment, population-serving employment, and households located by zone, the next step is to apply land absorption coefficients to each of the activities and to keep an accounting record of land use. Unusable land is first subtracted from the total land supply. It includes naturally unusable land—for example, land that is under water or too steep, and land preempted by public policy. Base-employment land use is supplied to PLUM and accepted without change. Population-serving–employment land use is assumed to preempt residential use. The residual land is available for residential use.

As is apparent from the description of the location of households, land availability is not considered as a constraint. Thus, it is possible that, given the land absorption coefficient for households, more land in any zone may be allocated than is actually available.

PLUM has a routine for reconciling the land allocated to residential use with the land available. First, present capacity in terms of number of households is defined by dividing the present stock of residential and vacant land by the residential land absorption matrix:

$$C^* = A_5{}^{-1}(a_5{}^* + a_8{}^*)$$

where C^* is the vector of residential capacities of zones, $a_5{}^*$ is the vector of present stock of residential land, $a_8{}^*$ is the vector of present stock of vacant land, and A_5 is the diagonal matrix of residential land absorption coefficients.

Next, two vectors of capacity utilization are defined. The first measures the initial capacity utilization; the second, the utilization after households have been allocated by PLUM:

$$y_i{}^* = h_i{}^*/C_i{}^*$$

$$x_i = h_i/C_i{}^*$$

where $h_i{}^*$ represents initial households in zone i, h_i, the projected households in zone i, $y_i{}^*$ is present capacity utilization in zone i, and x_i is the projected capacity utilization in zone i. While the elements of the vector y^* must be less than or equal to one, the elements of the vector x can be zero or any positive value. When any element of x is greater than one, more residential land is allocated to that zone than is available.

In order to reconcile the projected spatial distribution of housing units and their associated land requirements with the available supply of land in each zone, PLUM first defines two transformations of the elements of x:

$$y° = 1 - e^{-(e^x i^{-1})}$$

$$y_i{}^{°°} = 1 - e^{-(e^{2x} i^{-1})}.$$

Both $y_i{}°$ and $y_i{}^{°°}$ are always greater than or equal to zero, and less than one. Also, except when $x_i = 0$, $y_i{}^{°°}$ is greater than $y_i{}°$.

Zonal residential densities, and therefore zonal capacities, are adjusted in the model to reflect changes in residential demand. If $y_i{}°$ is greater than $y_i{}^*$, the proportion of capacity initially developed, the zonal residential density is adjusted as follows:

$$G_{i5}{}' = G_{i5}e^{m(v_i{}° - v_i{}^*)}$$

where G_{i5} is original residential density in zone i, m is density transformation coefficient, and $G_{i5}{}'$ is adjusted residential density in zone i. If $y_i{}°$ is less than $y_i{}^*$, G_{i5} is held constant. The density transformation coefficients are derived for each of the nine counties in the region using cross-section regression analysis.

The vector G_5 is used to define an adjusted zonal capacity, C' is G_5' $(a_5{}^* + a_8{}^*)$. Using this adjusted capacity and the previously derived constrained measures of the proportion of capacity developed, y° and $y^{\circ\circ}$, two vectors of zonal household allocations are derived: h° equals $y^{\circ}C^*$ and $h^{\circ\circ}$ equals $y^{\circ\circ}C'$.

The vector $h^{\circ\circ}$ is considered an "upper-limit allocation," and is used in the following definition:

$$W = 1 + \frac{1h - 1h^{\circ}}{1h^{\circ\circ} - 1h^{\circ}}.$$

W, a scalar, is used to derive a new vector of zonal development ratios,

$$x' = W \frac{h^{\circ}}{C'}.$$

The elements of this vector are then transformed to derive the final zonal development ratios:

$$y_i{}' = 1 - e^{-(e^{x'}{}_i{}^{-1})}.$$

Zonal household allocations are determined by $h'' = y'C'$.

This reallocation routine, of course, changes the spatial configuration of employed residents and nonworking residents. This requires the recalculation and adjustment of these variables to make zonal and areawide totals consistent.

OVERVIEW

Clearly, the BATS models have been designed to accommodate two often conflicting purposes of land-use modeling. First, of course, the models were designed to be an immediately useful planning tool. Second, they have been designed to allow the relatively easy introduction of the results of their continuing program of research on the behavior being modeled.

One area in which research would be of value is in the allocation of population-serving employment. It seems questionable to apply one areawide multiplier to all base employees and all families of base employees. Further, it seems questionable to suggest that the same multiplier will hold for workers at their working places and nonworkers at their residences. This assumption implies that employees do all their spending from their workplaces and that this spending generates the same multiplier as the rest of the family's per capita consumption from the place of residence. It is obvious that the results of future research on disaggregating the multiplier by worker type, working place, family income, family size, and residential location can be easily adapted for input into PLUM.

The model could also easily incorporate the results of research using the same kind of disaggregation for the home-to-work, work-to-shop, and home-to-shop allocation functions.

PLUM introduces changes in residential density with changes in the extent of land development, but no account is taken of changes in employment density. This asymmetry suggests that further extensions in this area might be fruitful.

9

Land-Use Modeling: Current Problems and Future Directions

THIS CHAPTER ATTEMPTS to identify and evaluate some of the major problems common to land-use modeling efforts. While the discussion relies heavily on the survey of land-use models for Atlanta, Southeastern Wisconsin, Detroit, Puget Sound, and the San Francisco-Oakland Bay Area presented earlier, it also draws on the study group's experience with land-use modeling in other metropolitan areas. In addition to the five areas mentioned, members of this study group have in-depth knowledge of land-use modeling activities in Chicago, Pittsburgh, Boston, and Philadelphia (Penn-Jersey); in London and Tyneside, England; Melbourne, Brisbane, Perth, and Adelaide, Australia; and in Tel Aviv and Haifa, Israel.

The following critique of land-use modeling divides logically into two parts. The first is concerned with technical and methodological problems; the second, with the difficulties of organizing research and building models for transportation planning.

TECHNICAL AND METHODOLOGICAL PROBLEMS

The earliest land-use models, such as those developed for the Detroit (1952) and Chicago (1956) transportation studies, used physical measures of land use—acres of land by type and square feet of building area. Recent studies, such as those surveyed for this study, are far more behavioral. They analyze and forecast employment and population levels. This is a major improvement. Still, the analysis is hampered by the virtual absence of data describing changes in metropolitan development at a useful level of disaggregation—by type of household, type of employment, or by location. In particular, insufficient effort has been made to model the underlying reasons for locational decisions by households and firms. Existing models would be better able to explain the changing pattern of urban growth if they paid more attention to these determinants.

It can be argued that there are important differences between structural models (those built to help us understand the processes of urban development) and forecasting models (those built to predict future development). Forecasting models, such as those described in this paper, may be adequate for many purposes as long as their predictions are accurate, even if they do not explain observed behavioral patterns. They are adequate, however, only so long as there are no major structural changes, for example, changes in zoning or the transportation network. In short, predictions made from mechanistic forecasting models might be able to reproduce the present locational patterns but still be incapable of predicting changes in location in a changing environment. Ultimately, the best forecasting model would be one that had a well-articulated behavioral or causal structure. But no truly satisfactory structural model of urban development has been developed as yet. Therefore, the case can still be made that a good forecasting model will provide better predictions than a poor structural model.

Cross-Sectional Bias

Any realistic lag structure designed to represent decisions as to land use or location almost surely spans many time periods. Physical investments in buildings, streets, sewers, and other urban structures are highly durable and, in general, are modified or abandoned slowly over time. Accordingly, the usual practice of estimating the factors influencing locational choice from a single cross section of data can result in substantial bias. Parameters developed from such cross-sectional studies can reproduce the existing location pattern, but are rarely suitable for modeling changes in land-use patterns over time.

In short, the existing land-use pattern is the result of decisions made over a considerable period and under varying historical conditions. The considerations affecting recent location decisions were probably different, or at least valued differently, from those that were important in earlier periods. Technological change is a major reason for the difference. For example, in the early 1900s most goods-producing industries receiving raw materials and other inputs from outside the urban area and shipping finished products to other areas would undoubtedly have located on a rail siding. Today many firms find truck transportation preferable and therefore are no longer as limited in their locational choices. Nonetheless, large numbers of such firms are located on rail sidings for historical reasons, and analysis of cross-section data may give this factor (accessibility to rail services) far more importance than it currently deserves.

Similar biases may result from technological changes within an industry. Changes in production, materials handling, and relative factor prices strongly favor single-level layouts for most manufacturing and wholesaling activities. These more spacious layouts require far more land space, and parking lots for employees' cars increase space requirements still more. Again, parameters estimated from cross-section samples tend to be averages of current and historical effects of land-space requirements, with the historical often predominating. Central cities contain few vacant sites large enough for modern plants, and the difficulties and cost of assembling sites all but prohibit the construction of new production facilities there. Still, central cities contain many industrial plants, and these dominate the cross-section analyses.

In general, the parameters derived from cross-section analysis will tend to produce forecasts that are more attuned to existing patterns than future ones. This results in assigning too large a portion of new activities to built-up areas and too small a portion to new or developing sectors of the urban area.[1] Existing activities tend to be returned to their present location despite real-world forces encouraging them to seek relocation. This predicted behavior is contradicted by time series data, which indicate that most new manufacturing plants are being built in suburban areas and existing firms are moving to new locations. Total employment at the original location may decline only slightly, remain stable, or even increase somewhat as a result of different activities moving into vacated space; however, the characteristics of the new employees may be considerably different from those of the old employees. To be roughly right in the aggregate may be insufficient for policy planners, who often need to understand the changes in composition and their causes.

To make accurate forecasts of locational decisions, it is necessary to

---

[1] For a further discussion of employment forecasting from cross-section data and a detailed critique of the Delaware Valley Planning employment allocation models (successor to Penn-Jersey), see John F. Kain, "The Location and Movement of Jobs and Industry," in *The Metropolitan Enigma: Inquiries into the Nature and Dimensions of America's "Urban Crisis,"* Cambridge, 1968.

understand the influence of various zonal characteristics that determine such changes over time. The use of time series data and changes in industry location may give parameter estimates that more adequately capture intertemporal changes in locational determinants. Backcasting (using the model to estimate location patterns in an earlier period), even at a more aggregate level, could provide a crude check on the stability of the parameters estimated from a single cross section and provide some indication of whether land-use determinants have changed. Where time series data have not been developed, which is all too commonly the case, models should be tested for their sensitivity to changes in the estimated cross-section parameters.

Interdependencies and Their Sequential Representation

Because urban systems are extremely complex, many variables and innumerable behavioral interrelationships and interdependencies seem relevant to land-use models. The first problem of modeling is to decide which of these relationships are important. To make this determination, we need to know a great deal more about the forces underlying urban development. And in order to formulate the interrelationships in sequential order, a substantial amount of experimentation and testing of hypotheses must be carried out. This implies extensive new research and increased communication between researchers and modelers.

After the important interrelationships have been specified, they must be incorporated into a model. The problem of conceptualizing and empirically estimating the interrelationships are greatly simplified if a sequential or recursive model structure is employed. Locational decisions are therefore represented, in most models, as sequential rather than simultaneous. Occasionally, an approximately simultaneous result is obtained by iterating a sequential set of relations.

In one of the models reviewed, for example, a family first decides on the type of housing it desires and then examines locations that offer this type of housing. It is clear that the real decision process is not so easily separated. If less attractive housing is available in a more desirable location, the decision might be made in the reverse order: location first, housing type second.

The order of the decisions can affect the characteristics of forecasts from the models. If the location preference is addressed first, the model would tend to forecast higher and higher densities (unless density constraints are used in the model), while the reverse ordering (housing type first) would tend to forecast lower densities.

The point of the above example is not to question the usefulness of the sequential technique or to suggest that reverse ordering of the decisions would produce a superior approximation. The point is, rather, that the representation of simultaneous or highly interdependent phenomena (such as housing type and location) is a necessary part of modeling and that it is a very sensitive and difficult problem. To a large extent, good modeling hinges on the ability to identify and represent such subtleties.

Industrial Location

All models surveyed recognize the critical importance of industrial location in determining metropolitan spatial structure and the location of households. Yet land-use modelers have devoted surprisingly little effort to analyzing the determinants of industrial location. It is actually only a slight exaggeration to claim that most existing land-use models are no more than models of residential location or population distribution. The location of basic industrial employment (as contrasted with retailing and service employment) is often determined ad hoc or simply based on the hopes and aspirations of the planners. Only a few planning efforts have made serious attempts to model the determinants of basic industrial location choices. For the most part these attempts have been quite limited and crude, particularly in behavioral content. Even worse from the standpoint of objectivity or scientific progress, analysts are often placed under great pressure to produce land-use–transportation studies that present projections favorable to the area or to some particular sector of the study area. This is seen most clearly in some employment projections for the CBDs of central cities. Organized groups, such as CBD associations, and political leaders are often concerned about the psychological effects of adverse projections. They can sometimes succeed in forcing study staffs to develop optimistic projections for certain sectors, against the staff's better judgment. Projection "errors" of this kind can cause large errors in capital investment choices in transportation. Consequently, there is much to be said for insulating the modeling and forecasting efforts from pressure groups.

Housing Stock Adjustments and Changes in the Character of Residential Areas

Most of the residential location–land-use models developed to date can be characterized as metropolitan growth or extension models. They have been primarily concerned with forecasting the extent and location of new peripheral development. Changes in built-up areas have been virtually ignored and there have been almost no attempts to systematically study or model the adjustment processes by which the stock of residential structures is adapted to new uses over time. Existing models have concentrated on explaining or projecting the determinants of housing demand and thereby have slighted the determinants of supply[2] and the effects of changes in demand on the housing stock and the character of areas.[3] Yet these adjustment processes are central to any analysis of housing markets.

New construction accounts for only a fraction of the housing supply during any time period and is sharply limited in its location. The relatively small body of research that exists on housing stock adaptation[4] is evidently not well known to those building land-use–transportation models and is not easily incorporated into existing models. Yet the changing of neighborhoods, especially in the central city, has a dramatic effect on several urban problems.

Housing Segregation: The Race Issue

Though its impact is not adequately understood, housing market discrimination has a substantial effect on metropolitan development. The residential location choices and travel patterns of nonwhites are dominated by segregation and seem to be markedly different from those of whites. Housing market discrimination affects housing prices and the attractiveness of various locations and thereby influences the residential location decisions and travel patterns of whites. Yet most land-use–transportation models fail to recognize race or the profound effects of discrimination.

One consequence of housing market discrimination is to make suburban jobs less accessible to Negroes segregated in central cities. In recent years there have been numerous proposals to improve access between the ghetto and suburban employment locations. The Department of Housing and Urban Development (HUD) and the Depart-

---

[2] The Southeastern Wisconsin model does try to simulate the supply of new housing by reflecting the independent decisions made by developers. The possible conversion of the existing housing stock was not addressed.

[3] One of the models did introduce a simple process for residential "filtering."

[4] Examples of investigations include Ira Lowry's formulation in "Filtering and Housing Standards: A Conceptual Analysis" in *Land Economics*, 36, No. 4, November 1960, using the economic investment approach; W. Grigsby's *Housing Markets and Public Policy*, Philadelphia, 1963; and W. Smith, *Filtering and Neighborhood Change*, Berkeley, 1964.

ment of Transportation (DOT) have several demonstration projects under way or in the planning stage. Although it has been hypothesized that the transportation gap between central city ghettos and suburban jobs is partially responsible for high Negro unemployment rates, these issues have not been considered in existing land-use–transportation studies.

Modeling Focus

The most useful models have been those built to answer particular questions. A model's form, the variables considered, and the time intervals used all depend heavily on the questions being asked. Thus far, there is no such thing as an all-purpose model to answer all questions about urban growth and development. Planners and modelers must therefore agree on what questions should be dealt with.

For instance, planners and model builders must determine whether a specific model should be directed toward defining future conditions or toward understanding the transition from a current to a future condition. The two objectives may require different model structures and certainly use different time intervals to forecast the spatial distribution of activity. Traditionally, transportation planners have been concerned primarily with designing an "optimal transport system for the future." The models then were developed to forecast future land use in some target year with no regard for the pattern developing in the intervening years or the effect of transportation investment decisions on this development. Similarly, there has been little or no attention paid to the adequacy of the transportation system in the intervening years, or to the best phasing of transport investments.

Testing the Models

Another issue is the extent to which transportation planners have accepted the land-use forecasts as accurate and error-free. Because of the models' admitted shortcomings, it is most important that tests be made of the sensitivity of the results to different control totals and parameter estimates. Both trip forecasts and land-use forecasts should be tested in this manner.

No one will ever invent a method for making perfect forecasts of regional employment and population. Thus the standard question "How much error is acceptable?" can be answered only in terms of how much of the model's projection of land use is affected by changes in inputs and whether planners consider the resulting variance in the land-use projections as acceptable. Furthermore, sensitivity tests for changes in the level of parameters or changes in the form of equations would provide valuable insights into the model's robustness.

Continuous study and planning at the local level facilitates the process of testing and updating. One might expect that time series data, so desperately needed for urban studies, would be developed from such efforts. This ongoing process of analysis should identify presently unrecognized trends and relationships. As the models are modified on the basis of new data, their forecasting accuracy and structural content should increase. Only in this way—continually testing against new data, respecification, and reestimation—will truly useful models be developed.

PROBLEMS IN ORGANIZATION, PLANNING, AND THE STATE OF THE ART OF MODELING

Organizational Problems Affecting Modeling

The quality and relevance of land-use modeling in transportation planning crucially depend on the competence of the professional staff and the organization of the research and planning activities. Local planning agencies have increasingly employed transportation and planning consultants to develop their land-use models and transportation plans. Over the years several of these firms have acquired a great deal of experience and developed skilled transportation planning teams. A few very large consulting firms have experts in most of the problem areas associated with transportation and land-use planning, but in most cases the needed skills and knowledge are widely scattered. Consultants tend to specialize in certain parts of the overall problem. Therefore, a decision to hire consultants to construct a land-use model often implies a decision to fragment the modeling effort by giving it to several different consultants.

Currently, modeling is much more a problem of design than of production. It relies heavily on trial and error. As new ways of specifying the interrelationships are developed, the design of the overall model is modified and remodified. The model structure tends to be continually redefined and efforts are constantly redirected toward newly discovered critical areas. For the model to be effective, however, the various submodels must be internally consistent and the final model must be an appropriate "aggregation" of the different individual efforts. This implies extensive interaction among developers of the individual submodels or components. When a modeling effort is fragmented among several consultants, this is exceedingly difficult to achieve, and it is often necessary to force the several submodels together in a highly unsatisfactory manner.

Some local agencies try to solve the problem of model coordination by contracting the entire modeling effort to a single consultant. Thus, the problem of articulating the several components of the model is solved, but planning agencies using this approach are likely to end up with a model that is a complete mystery to them. Consequently, the local planning agency will generally be unable to modify the model to reflect new information. It will be even less able to alter the structure of the model or the techniques used in its construction. As parts of continuing studies, such models are likely to be useful only for the initial forecasts. For future planning or altering existing plans, the planning agency will either have to return to the consultant who developed the model originally, develop its own models, or simply make do without modeling assistance.

Furthermore, when models are developed completely by consultants, the local agency misses the improved understanding that comes from having to carefully specify, examine, and evaluate the important forces behind urban development. It is indeed a significant loss, since one of the greatest benefits obtained from the construction of land-use models is the understanding or learning from experience gained by the builders in the process of actually constructing the model.

In short, there are strong arguments for having the local planning group develop the models. In order to build such a model local planners would be forced to examine the structure of their community and seek to identify and quantify the forces affecting their area. The experience and insight gained by this exercise would be immensely valuable to any continuing planning program. Having local planners do the modeling would also increase the likelihood that variables and emphasis, particularly important to the specific area, would be introduced into the models. It is possible that the resulting models might be less sophisticated than those developed by consultants; however, the involvement and experience gained by the local group could far outweigh the disadvantages of not having a more sophisticated or innovative model. Of course, in building the model, the local planning staff might well draw on the special skills of consultants and thus take advantage of the best current techniques. The difficulty with the present practice is that consultants all too often replace local planning agencies rather than assist them in planning. Of course, a decision to build models locally may also imply that planning staffs must be upgraded in technical and quantitative skills.

At present, in most local planning programs a rather confused and uneasy combination of goals can be identified. Local areas want models useful for their planning programs. The better consultants, on the other hand, are chiefly interested in advancing the state of the art, and therefore may view the local planning studies principally as an opportunity to accomplish their research. Within the present institutional framework, the goals of planning and research are often competitive rather than complementary.

Ideally, research and development should be continued, but not as part of planning studies. Researchers might have more success in increasing the body of knowledge about the processes of urban development if they were relieved of the severe deadline pressures of particular planning programs. Besides, if the two goals were further separated, models more appropriate to local planning purposes might be developed and a better and more lasting relationship between researchers and planners achieved.

Documentation

Evaluation of the land-use models developed for public agencies is made extremely difficult by their limited documentation. None of the studies considered in this survey provided sufficient information about the structure, weaknesses and shortcomings, or predictive ability of their models to permit a comprehensive review or evaluation. This is true not only of the widely distributed final reports but also of the supposedly more detailed technical papers and memoranda. The study group encountered large and critical gaps in the descriptions of the models. Only extensive follow-up and discussions with the planning staffs (who, however, gave generously of their time in these efforts) made it possible to make any headway in filling these gaps.

The extraordinary amount of time and effort necessary to interpret, define, and understand current work in land-use modeling makes any substantial interchange of ideas between workers in this field very difficult. Advances as well as mistakes are lost in present documentation. Conversely, some failures result in such bad publicity that a basically sound approach is abandoned. Clearly, improved communication and documentation are prerequisites for accelerating advances in modeling efforts.

It is not hard to explain why there is such a serious lack of adequate documentation. The modelers are faced with an extremely difficult assignment and are under strong pressures to get results. Under these conditions it would be surprising if they allocated much of their limited budgets and resources to the time-consuming job of carefully documenting all their efforts. In addition, many model builders, wishing to give the best possible impression of their work, gloss over the problems and present their effort as a polished and perfected product. This "sales requirement" leads to a different presentation than that required for the systematic and efficient long-run development of the basic techniques. The problem arises both from the difficulty of evaluating the quality of work in an area of this kind and the general lack of technical competence of clients. Many model builders obviously feel that if they honestly explain the problems and limitations of their necessarily primitive and incomplete models, the clients will fail to appreciate the models' usefulness or will hire consultants who promise more.

To be of real value in advancing the state of the art, a report on a specific model must present considerable detail and clearly identify weaknesses and shortcomings as well as strengths. The models' problems should be pointed out in the reports, and methods used by the model builders to handle these problems should be extensively discussed. In most cases, the really tough problem areas are common to all these efforts; progress in handling them will require a great deal of communication among model builders.

The use of profit-making consultants introduces additional problems of communicating research findings and empirical methods. There are good reasons why profit-making consultants cannot be expected to improve the documentation process. Many regard their modeling expertise as privileged and feel that disclosing such information could affect their competitive position. One consultant said that his reports had been intentionally written in an obscure manner. He explained that his company had been working some twenty years to develop its approach and he saw no reason to release such information. He did not see his firm as having any responsibilities for educating others in the development and use of land-use models.

Other consultants view documentation as a way of advertising their abilities and seem quite willing to include extensive explanations of modeling innovations. Unfortunately, their audience often neither requires nor desires the details considered necessary by other researchers. The step-by-step procedures and the results of each calibration effort are expensive to document and produce little in the way of advertising returns. It is also true that failures are commonly omitted and modest successes presented in the most favorable light.

Neither of the above situations questions the honesty or integrity of the consultant. Rather, the comments reflect the need for an incentive structure that encourages adequate documentation and its widespread distribution. To a limited extent, professional associations and agencies such as the Highway Research Board disseminate research findings and information on innovations in model building. However, such outlets are inadequate. The type of documentation required is usually too bulky to be accepted for publication or public presentation by such organizations. Only the more important and successful innovations are ever presented at meetings or in the journals. Even then, the paper or article is more likely to be couched in theoretical terms, with only summary attempts at practical application or specific testing. And since no honor is attached to reporting a failure, honest but doomed attempts are repeated again and again, often at considerable expense.

To offset some of these problems, sponsoring agencies commonly dispatch representatives for periodic monitoring. This has tended to produce documentation suitable only to the scope of the monitoring agency's interests. Usually, funding agencies are more interested in successfully completing the contract than in disseminating information; hence, the reports are often of limited use in advancing the state of the art.

One possible solution might be to employ "reporters" to follow and thoroughly document each study. This could be done by transportation consultants, university faculty, or similarly qualified persons. It should be emphasized that their function and responsibility would not be research, but carefully detailed reporting and documentation of methods and important innovations. They would be responsible for reviewing all documents, published and unpublished, produced by the study staff and for obtaining clarification of poorly documented material. Continuity is of the utmost importance in this function. Ideally, these reporters would be assigned to particular studies from conception to completion. Federally financed planning groups would be required to cooperate fully with the reporters and to make copies of all internal and external documents available to them.

A major difficulty of this reportorial approach, however, is that it would underutilize the knowledge and skills of the analysts actually engaged in research. The analyst is the one most capable of documenting his work and providing detailed discussions of methodology and empirical findings. What is needed are incentives to insure that analysts and study staffs give adequate attention to documentation. It might be argued that this could be accomplished by including funds for better documentation in the budgets of study agencies. This incentive already exists to some degree, although it does not seem to have been very successful. The study staffs tend to use the additional funds for further analysis and research, and continue to skimp on documentation. The difficulty is that documentation and adequately written presentations on the methodology and findings take more effort and are less satisfying than actual analysis. Incentives for complete documentation simply do not exist.

Another possible solution is to have an outside agency act as a research monitor. Under this approach, the funding federal agencies might make an appropriate nonprofit organization, such as the Urban Institute, responsible for documentation. The local planning groups would be required to document all their modeling and submit the information to the monitoring agency. This agency (e.g., the Institute) would judge whether the documentation is adequate. Should the monitoring agency consider it inadequate, it would be empowered to require the local planning group to provide further information.

An arrangement of this kind might considerably improve the quality of documentation. Furthermore, with the collection centralized in one agency, one would expect more of a systematic review and a more efficient distribution of reports.

The most obvious difficulty with this suggestion is that to be successful the operation depends largely on a working relationship between local planning groups and the research monitor. The extent to which the monitor is taken seriously by the planning groups depends, in part, on the lead taken by the federal government. The funding agency must recognize the importance of documentation and make its concern clear to the local groups.

The responsibilities of the monitoring organization must be clearly defined. The monitor, for instance, should not see its role as evaluating the researchers' efforts, nor should the researchers feel that the monitor is evaluating them.

Basic Research

Many of the problems described above result from uncertainties about how to structure land-use modeling, and from a general lack of knowledge about the behavioral determinants and processes of metropolitan development. A good deal of basic research is needed to determine the relevant variables and important relationships.

The present stage of development in land-use modeling and the relatively limited emphasis on basic research reflect the incentive structure implicit in federal grants-in-aid programs for land-use and transportation planning. These incentives encourage particular cities and their consultants to analyze exhaustively their own problems. The state of the art has been advanced slowly through these ongoing planning efforts, as permitted by budgets and the competence of consultants. In fact, with the present incentive structure, it is remarkable that so much progress has occurred. Research and modeling have been, to a considerable extent, "bootleg efforts," continually forced to justify their role within the planning effort. Because of the pressures of the planning process, research has necessarily been slighted.

Experimentation and real research is accompanied by high risks. It is difficult to expect planning agencies or consultants to undertake these risks in view of the rather specific requirements to produce an operational model or a forecast within a limited time period. Still, only through progress in basic research can progress in transportation modeling and planning be expected.

TOTAL COST AND ALLOCATION OF STUDY BUDGETS

Comprehensive urban transportation studies vary greatly in terms of total costs. The costs depend primarily on the size of the metropolitan area and the complexity of the study design. Costs tend to go up as study designs become more comprehensive and sophisticated. The trend toward larger study budgets was accentuated in 1961, when legislation was amended to make Housing and Home Finance (HUD) "701" funds available for transportation planning. The "701" funds could be used for somewhat broader purposes than the "1½ per cent" highway funds, which had been the principal source of financing for "comprehensive" urban transportation studies before 1961. The "701" funds, in particular, permitted a substantial expansion in the collection of land-use statistics and in the scope of land-use modeling.

While precise cost data are not available because of many difficult problems of imputation and consistency of definition, the six studies considered in this survey ranged in cost between an estimated $1.77 million (Puget Sound) and $5.54 million (Bay Area Transportation

Study). Most available cost estimates for "comprehensive" transportation studies must be regarded as lower-bound estimates representing forecast budgets rather than actual expenditures. Invariably, the costs of these studies exceed their estimates by a large margin. For example, the original cost projection for the Penn-Jersey study was $2.45 million; more recently Zettle and Carll placed the costs of this study at $4.5 million.[5] The higher figure is still only an estimate since the study is not completed—there will probably be further cost increases before it is finished.

Comprehensive metropolitan transportation studies are costly undertakings. The "expenses" can be seen in a more reasonable perspective by recognizing that the $2 million to $6 million cost of a major transportation study is about equivalent to the cost of one mile of a centrally located freeway.

The high costs of metropolitan transportation studies can be attributed primarily to the large-scale surveys used to obtain travel data. For example, the *Prospectus* of the Penn-Jersey Transportation Study,[6] one of the most detailed presentations of study costs available, provides $610,000 for home interviews alone. Projected data collection costs for Penn-Jersey rise to just under $1 million when the truck-taxi, roadside-survey, and screen-line counts are added. This budget does not include anything for key punching, tabulating, or processing the hundreds of thousands of trip records obtained from the surveys. The estimated costs of these data preparation and processing operations amount to nearly another one-half million dollars. Up-to-date budgets on actual expenditures for the Penn-Jersey study have not been published. However, $2 million is probably not a bad estimate of the actual total cost of collecting and processing the trip data. These $2 million include no funds to develop behavioral models for explaining present and forecasting future traffic, and no funds for collecting and processing land-use data. They cover only the collection, preparation, and initial processing of trip data. Furthermore, the Penn-Jersey expenditures appear to have been exceeded by the Bay Area Transportation Study (BATS). The BATS report of actual outlays, as of December 31, 1968, estimated total expenditures for its home interview survey at $1,609,023 (including data preparation and basic data

[5] Richard M. Zettle and Richard R. Carll, "Summary Review of Major Metropolitan Area Transportation Studies in the United States," Berkeley, November 1962.

[6] Philadelphia, December 11, 1959, pp. 19–21.

reduction). An additional $478,528 was spent for roadside interviews, and $82,664 was spent on a truck-taxi survey.

In comparison to the sums allocated to the collection and basic processing of trip data, the budgets of these "comprehensive" urban transportation studies for developing land-use models and forecasts are inadequate. The Penn-Jersey *Prospectus* allocates only $8,000 to studies of employment patterns and trends by industry and area, and $16,000 to analyses of industry location factors. These analyses were to be based on a program of land-use data collection estimated at $50,000. Again, actual expenditures may have been considerably larger than those budgeted. Nevertheless, if changes in land use are as crucial to transportation planning as our previous arguments suggest, study allocations for the development of land-use models appear seriously inadequate.

It should be noted, however, that the Penn-Jersey transportation study devoted far greater resources (both absolutely and relative to its total budget) to collecting land-use data and developing land-use models than any of the earlier studies and all but a few of the more recent ones. Thus, the pattern of expenditures of most other "comprehensive" urban transportation studies is even less advantageous to analytical efforts than that of the Penn-Jersey study.

Specifically, the experience of the major studies considered in this survey does not appear to depart markedly from that described for Penn-Jersey. Less detailed budget data were available for these five studies, but a crude breakdown of expenditures for them is presented in Table 8. The percentages should be thought of only as reasonable approximations. Even so, the data support a rather consistent expenditure pattern, which is quite similar to the one found by Zettle and Carll in a survey of metropolitan transportation studies.[7] While the fractions may not be precise, the heavy allocations for data collection and basic processing dominate the study budgets.

Estimates of the direct costs of land-use modeling were available for some of the studies. Southeastern Wisconsin spent about $125,000 (6.2 per cent of total), and the Bay Area (BATS) about $228,000 (4.7 per cent of total). These cost estimates exclude data collection and only represent expenditures for the design and calibration of the models. (Southeastern Wisconsin has undertaken further model designs since preparation of this report; those expenditures are not included in the above total.)

[7] Zettle and Carll, "Summary Review," 1962.

Table 8
Transportation Study Budget

Atlanta Study (1961–68)	
Total budget[a]	$1.75 million
Data collection and processing	36%
Analysis and models	24%
Planning functions	34%
Miscellaneous projects	6%
Southeastern Wisconsin Study (1963–66)	
Total budget[a]	$1.99 million
Data collection and processing	62%
Analysis and models	14%
Planning functions	16%
Miscellaneous projects	8%
Bay Area Transportation Study (1968 on)	
Total budget	$5.54 million
Data collection and processing	60%
Analysis and models	18%
Planning functions	14%
Miscellaneous projects	8%
Detroit TALUS (1968 on)	
Total budget	$4.70 million
Data collection and processing	46%
Analysis and models	19%
Planning functions	20%
Miscellaneous projects	15%
Puget Sound Transportation Study (1960 on)	
Total budget[a,b]	$1.77 million

NOTE: These budgets and their breakdowns are approximate. Percentages shown, while based on actual budgets, are judgmentally derived because of classification problems.

[a] This total is an estimate of the entire project which was completed before January 1, 1969.

[b] Further breakdown is not available.

The estimated total study costs shown in Table 8 must be regarded with a certain caution and the percentages must be approached with even greater reserve.

But even if there are errors in the estimated costs presented in the table, it is obvious that the dominant cost in these studies has been that of gathering and reducing original data. Earlier (i.e., pre-1960) studies allocated, on the average, about two-thirds of their budgets for this function. With the availability of "701" funds, the growing recognition of the importance of land-use modeling, and the establishment of continuing planning agencies, this proportion has been reduced to approximately one-half.

Selected Sources

CHAPTER 3—PUGET SOUND REGIONAL TRANSPORTATION STUDY

Unless otherwise specified, the following papers are available through the Puget Sound Regional Planning Commission, Seattle, which is the successor to the Transportation Study.

Grave, C. H., "Forecasting the Distribution of 1985 Population and Employment to Analysis Zones for Plan A," Staff Report No. 15, 1964.

Joshi, R. N., "Distribution of 1985 Population and Employment to Analysis Zones for Land Use Plan B," Staff Report No. 17, 1964.

Joshi, R. N., and Utevesky, R., "Alternative Patterns of Development—Puget Sound Region," mimeo., 1964.

Little, Arthur D., "Economic Growth of the Puget Sound Region," mimeo., 1964.

"Population Projections for the Puget Sound Region," mimeo., Puget Sound Governmental Conference and Regional Planning Conference, October 1960. (Revised: September 1962, May 1963.)

CHAPTER 4—SOUTHEASTERN WISCONSIN REGIONAL PLANNING COMMISSION STUDY

The following papers are available through the Southeastern Wisconsin Regional Planning Commission, Milwaukee.

A Land Use Plan Design Model: Volume One—Model Development, Technical Report No. 8, January 1968.

A Mathematical Approach to Urban Design—A Progress Report on a Land Use Plan Design Model and a Land Use Simulation Model, Technical Report No. 3, January 1966.

The Regional Economic Simulation Model, Technical Report No. 5, October 1966.

Planning Reports: Recommended Regional Land-Use–Transportation Plans—1960, November 1966; *Inventory Findings—1963,* October 1966; *Forecasts and Alternative Plans—1990,* October 1966.

CHAPTER 5—ATLANTA REGION METROPOLITAN PLANNING

"Atlanta Area Transportation Study: Existing Conditions Report," mimeo, State Highway Department of Georgia, 1967.

People, Jobs, and Land, Population and Economy Report No. 1, available from the Atlanta Region Metropolitan Planning Commission, Atlanta. The latter is also a source for the following mimeo. reports (circa 1964): "1983 Labor Force"; "1983 Family Income"; "1983 Population Distribution by Age Groups"; "1983 Employment Distribution"; "1983 Non-Institutional Population"; "1983 Occupied Housing Units and Net Residential Densities"; "1983 Retail Trade Sales and Floor Space and Retail Service Floor Space."

CHAPTER 6—DETROIT REGIONAL TRANSPORTATION AND LAND-USE STUDY

Rubin, I. J. "TALUS: The Detroit Regional Transportation and Land Use Study," *Proceedings of the IEEE,* April 1968.

Data from TALUS, Detroit Regional Transportation and Land-Use Study, Detroit, 1967.

TALUS and Tomorrow, Detroit Regional Transportation and Land-Use Study, Detroit, 1968.

TALUS Working Paper Number 2, CONSAD Research Corporation, Pittsburgh, 1968.

An Urban-Regional Model of Small Area Change for Southeastern Michigan, CONSAD Research Corporation, Pittsburgh, July 1969.

CHAPTER 7—BAY AREA SIMULATION STUDY

Jobs, People and Land: Bay Area Simulation Study Special Report Number 6, Center for Real Estate and Urban Economics, Institute of Urban Regional Development, Berkeley, 1968.

CHAPTER 8—BAY AREA TRANSPORTATION STUDY

Goldner, William, *Projective Land Use Model (PLUM),* Bay Area Transportation Study Commission, BATSC Technical Report 219, September 1968.

"BATSC Locational Model System," Bay Area Transportation Study Commission, August 1968.

"EMPRO: BATSC Employment Projections—San Francisco Bay Area: Nine Counties 1965–1990," Bay Area Transportation Study Commission, April 1968.

INDEX